Always Connected
For Those Who Have Lost Children
Children Give Signs & Insights from Heaven

By
Joseph M. Higgins

Part of the Always Connected Series

Always Connected:
For Those Who Have Lost Children
Children Give Signs & Insights from Heaven

Copyright © 2020 Joseph M. Higgins
Always Connected, LLC
All Rights Reserved

No part of this book may be reproduced or transmitted in any form or by any means without written permission from the author.

Editorial design and illustrations by Gerard Galvis.

ISBN-13: 978-0-9825716-3-7

Printed in U.S.A.

Disclaimer

The information offered in this book does not constitute a substitute for professional treatment, therapy, or other types of professional advice and intervention. If expert advice or counseling is needed, the services of a competent professional should be sought.

The information contain in this book is solely the opinion of the author and his Spiritual Guides and should not be considered as a form of therapy, advice, direction, and/or diagnosis or treatment of any kind.

This book is available at quantity discounts for bulk purchases.
For information, please contact www.joehiggins.com

Dedication

This book is dedicated to all those who have been connected to the loss of a child of any age. May this book bring some insights about their passing and bring you peace and healing, knowing they are still around you and that you will see them again.

Remember you are *Always Connected.*

Acknowledgments

I would like to thank the children who brought through great insights to allow all of us to learn from their perspective that they are still involved in our lives and wish to see us enjoying our futures. I am grateful to them for sending signs to their loved ones and allowing others to read about their contact and know that life does continue after the change called death.

I would like to acknowledge all the people who supplied sign stories for this book. By allowing me to share your stories, you will help bring peace and healing to those who read about your personal, loving connections—now and in the future.

Special thanks to JoJo and Jen for their support on this project and for introducing me to their beautiful children in spirit, Karla and Kevin. Both children have taught me many things about the transition of a child as well as about life itself. Their knowledge and insights will help many in their struggle to understand the passing of a child.

As always, I need to thank my teachers and guides for helping me with the presentation, information, and insights found in this book. Without your continuous support, this book would not have been possible. We are truly *Always Connected.*

Andrew

Approximately fifteen years ago, I was driving in my car. I had just gone through a drive-through fast food restaurant and stopped to have lunch. All of a sudden, I felt a presence trying to communicate with me. This doesn't usually happen because I set up guidelines about the proper time to connect with me. At this particular time, a young man started to come through with the intention of trying to let his sister know he was okay. He was clear in his connection, and the information was coherent in nature.

He wanted me to contact his sister to let her know he was okay.

The young man began to tell me about his life and started to list things. I realized very quickly that I would not be able to remember all the details, so I began to write them down. I had to use the napkins that came in my lunch bag because the information was coming through so quickly that I didn't have time to seek out regular notebook paper.

So, as I began to scribble this information, I realized that it might indeed be possible to connect with his sister or possibly another loved one to pass the message along that this young man was okay on the other side. Below is some of the information that came through, totally unexpected, that afternoon.

The young man's name is Andrew. He was in college and was coming back from a game between the University of Kentucky and the University of Tennessee. I'm not sure which of these schools he attended. I saw the team colors and realized these were both big sports schools and sensed the two were celebrating. He was not driving at the time of his death because he was too drunk to drive. Unfortunately, his girlfriend, who was the driver, had also been drinking, and they were involved in an accident that took his life.

Andrew went to high school in Texas—I believe in the Dallas area. He was a scholar athlete and, I believe, a valedictorian.

His sister lived in the Midwest and traveled for a living. I had the feeling that she may have been a stewardess for an airline or perhaps a tour guide. She was divorced, and I don't know whether she was still working at the time of his passing.

Over the years, I have reached out to a few people to see if I could find anyone who may have known Andrew or perhaps his sister.

I wanted to include this incident in this book, as I thought it was very appropriate, and I hope that perhaps someone who reads this might recognize some of the details.

These things happen once in a while, and it is usually very difficult to locate the living relatives, but having this opportunity to talk about children passing, I thought I would give it a shot. If anyone has information concerning this story, please contact me. I would love to discuss any information you might have. Thank you.

Table of Contents

Section I: Introduction 1
    The *Always Connected* Series. 3
    Who I Am & Why This Book. 5
    Guides & Why This Subject. 10
    The Process. 18

Section II: The Bigger Picture. 23
    Who Is A Child 25
    Why They Left. 30
    Soul, Life Plans & Free Will 34
    Time, Perspective & Access Points 38
    Exit Points. 44
    When a Child Passes. 48
    Transitional Stories. 52
    Sign Stories
        Soul Group 59
        The Light 60
        The Moon. 62
        Finding Each Other 63
        His Voice 64
        Giving Blood. 66

Section III: Relationships 69
    Group Grief 71
    Interactions with Others. 75
    Discussing with Other Children 80
    Children's Insights 84
    Sign Stories
        Everyone Gets a Shirt. 89
        Sibling Signs 90
        Blinking Lights 91
        Sign In the Clouds 93
        A Heart. 94
        Ribbons 95
        The Rose. 97

Section IV: Guilt & Suicide **99**
   Guilt. 101
   Could I Have Done Something Differently?. 103
   Suicide. 107
   Parents & Suicide. 112
   Children's Insights to Parents on Suicide 118
   Sign Stories
      The Globe. 124
      Wash Your Guilt Away 125
      My Drink & a Laugh 127
      Baseball & Numbers. 128
      Phone Call 129
      Sense of Humor 130
      GPS 131

Section V: Transitioning **135**
   Illness 137
   Violence & the Passing of a Child. 142
   Murder 149
   Addictions 159
   Insights into Addiction. 164
   Abortion & Miscarriage 173
   Sign Stories
      A Literal Sign 177
      Feathers & a Birthday 178
      Blue Bird 180
      Still Taking Care 182
      Every Night. 182
      The Word, Not The Sound 183
      My Beautiful Butterfly. 184

Section VI: Signs 187
- The Language 189
- The Importance of Signs...................... 193
- Is It Authentic?............................. 198
- Methods 200
- Children's Insights 206
- *Sign Stories*
  - Dreams................................... 212
  - The Butterflies.......................... 214
  - Sounds & Cardinals....................... 214
  - Pennies & Lights......................... 216
  - The Kingfisher........................... 217
  - License Plate & Image 218
  - Mom Needs a New Phone 219

Section VII: Healing............................ 221
- Love Is Infinite............................. 223
- Healing Through Health 227
- Connecting with Our Side 235
- Pets & Healing............................... 238
- Coping Mechanisms............................ 242
- Nature....................................... 245
- Music.. 247
- *Sign Stories*
  - Music 249
  - The Blue Jay & Cardinal 250
  - A Favorite Artist........................ 252
  - Go Team & "21" 253
  - Feathers 254
  - The Red Light 255
  - The Announcement 256
- Final Word 257
- Soul Reference Guide 259
- Reference Quotes to Help You Heal............ 261

Section VIII: Resources 275

Section I

Introduction

*"We are not human beings on a spiritual journey.
We are spiritual beings on a human journey."*

Pierre Teilhard de Chardin
1881-1955
French Philosopher and Jesuit Priest

The *Always Connected* Series

I wanted to add this book to the *Always Connected Series* because it is a great example of how our loved ones, even though physically gone, are still connected to all of us here. It is a great example of how death cannot separate the loving connection we share with our family and friends. I hope you enjoy the information contained in this series as well as the stories that have been so generously supplied in order to help bring insight, peace, and healing into your life.

The following is an explanation from my guides of how we are always connected.

[Channeled from Joe's guides] I got your message

We want to convey to everyone the knowledge that each and every one of you is always connected. You are all connected on a spiritual level. And yes, you are all connected on a physical level. On a physical level, you all share the same physical plane. At this time, you all live on a living structure you call Earth; in the future, you will share life on other structures. Your physical bodies basically consist of all the same elements, so there are many common connections between you and every other physical being with whom you interact.

On a spiritual level, which is much broader than the physical level, you share similar attributes. You share a similar spiritual existence. The makeup of your spiritual being is similar to that of others with whom you interact, and your ability to learn and create experiences is similar to that of others.

So not only are you connected on the physical and spiritual levels, but you must also realize that at no time are you alone. We realize that there are times in people's lives when they feel as if they're totally alone, both physically and spiritually. This is never the case. You are always interacting with others, either physically or spiritually and either consciously or subconsciously.

Your spiritual entities are in constant contact with others on our plane who help guide you through your existence and journey on the Earth plane. There is never a time when you are alone on your journey and do not have access to help from others on our plane. You are always connected, you always have been connected, and you always will be connected.

Who I Am & Why This Book

My name is Joe Higgins, and I am a medium, channeler, and researcher. I have been given an extraordinary opportunity to communicate with those who have passed to the other side and have witnessed the connection and love that continue after the change we call death. In recent years, I have focused on channeling information from guides and teachers in order to bring this much-needed information to the Earth plane. I am humbled that during this life, I can make a difference in someone's life and perhaps even make a difference in the development of knowledge throughout the world.

There seems to be a lot of information written about the connection we have from our side to the other side. Yet oftentimes many questions remain, especially about certain subjects. One of these subjects is the crossing of a child.

It seems as though there's an awful lot of information out there but not too much that talks about how things work in a situation when a child passes. We know we can communicate with them through mediumship, and we know they send signs to let us know they're still around. But I thought it was necessary to ask some of the serious questions that torment people when losing a child.

I felt the need to write on this topic because I found it challenging that we couldn't get firm answers on this particular subject. We get bits and pieces from various sources, such as mediums and others who are able to connect with the other side, but I thought the information needed to all be in one place. I had success in connecting with deceased veterans for my veterans book, *Always Connected for Veterans: Deceased Vets Give Guidance from the Other Side,* so I thought that by contacting some of the children who have passed over, I could access some useful information that could then be shared with parents as well as anyone else who had been connected to and then lost a child.

From being a practicing medium for over twenty years, I have accumulated a good amount of knowledge from some of the children who have come through the readings. As with most of my readings, I asked questions about the bigger picture of life and aspects of the other side while trying to access pieces of the puzzle that we call life and death. Many times this information is transferred to me during one of these sittings. I believe this research gives us valuable insights into who we really are and why this life is so special.

A lot of the information that has come through was a learning experience for me as well as the person I was giving the reading to. After the reading, and sometimes right in the middle of it, I would tell someone to remember that particular piece of information, as sometimes my short-term memory becomes extremely limited. The reason I ask is because some of what comes through is information I had never heard about or something that clarifies some of the information we generally know now.

An example of this is exit points. Many people have read about or heard of the term *exit points*. During one reading with a little girl named Karla, she showed me exactly how an exit point works (which I will explain later in the book). I was so fascinated with the explanation she gave me that I told her mom that information would be put in a book at some point to help others realize that there are more things at play when a young person passes over. It's one of the main reasons I decided to write this book—because this information can bring healing and insight to those who suffer the loss of a child.

So, I began to ask questions about certain situations when I had brought through a child. Many times when a child comes through during a reading, they come through pretty strongly. Their energy is high, and information seems to flow more easily than with some adults.

One such reading concern the passing of a young man from suicide. After providing some evidence of who was coming through, Kevin tried to explain to his mother the circumstances of his passing. The information that came through was fascinating to me, and I also thought to myself that it must be shared with other parents who have lost children.

This book was originally scheduled to be written back in 2013. I began to gather information and put together an outline of questions I wanted to ask to see if I could get some insights in order to help people. The book was put on hold as I realized that the continuing loss of lives during the Afghanistan War, both on the battlefield and at home through suicide, needed to be addressed.

So, over the course of seven days, it was determined that the veterans book needed to be written right away. As a result, I put the children's book on the back burner. And over the years when I returned to collecting information about children, one reason or another caused the book to come to a halt. However, as the years went on, I acquired more information, and I realized it was time to put it all together and make it public.

Some of my notes are from 2015 and 2016. One of the outlines I was using was called "Parents Book 2016." Now it's called "Parents Book 2020." But actually, as I was switching the name of my outline from 2016 to 2020, I took out the word *Parents* and replaced it with *For Those*. Through the years, I've learned that the interaction between an adult and child does not have to be biological or even within the extended family. Many relationships are fostered throughout a child's life, and the adults who are part of this will often suffer tremendously when the child passes. Mentors, coaches, neighbors, and anyone who might have influenced or experienced the growth of the child over a period of years becomes attached to that soul. When the child passes, some of these people who were outside the family circle believe they have to hide or tone down their grief since they were not family members. Some may experience guilt for their feelings as they begin to judge themselves as not being as important as a family member.

So the word *parents* was removed, and the more general wording was put into the title. And as you will see in the book, people outside the family can be an important source of healing when interacting with close family members.

So, the overall aim of the book is to bring information and insights into the larger picture when a younger person crosses over and how we react to such a situation. The age of the child is also not as significant as one may think. A middle-aged adult is still considered a child to an elderly parent or sibling.

I also wanted to make sure the book could be directed to as wide a group as possible since people are at many different levels of development as well as different stages in their grief process. Some of the information may resonate with some, while it may not make any sense to others. Some people might be focused on certain parts of the book more than others.

I saw how this worked out when I wrote the veterans book, as parts of the book focused on different type of veterans from different wars. They wanted to be able to reach *all* veterans—now as well as from future conflicts. So universality was another goal I wanted to achieve in this book.

I hope people understand that there really is a bigger picture going on in all of our lives. Things are not always as they seem. We put expectations on all parts of our lives. When we do this, we are surprised when things do not play out as we had planned. But in actuality, the true plan is playing out, with the finer details being our free will.

It is so true when we hear the expression "Life is short." In our linear world of time, it *can* be short. The expression should instead be: "Life is short on the Earth plane" because in actuality, life continues on after our physical death, just as it was continuing back before our birth.

I hope you gain insight from this book and that it brings you some healing and peace. That is its purpose. Take what you need and share it with others who may be suffering, and you will create a healing wave that can ripple around the world.

Guides & Why This Subject

※※※

When I started writing my first book, Hello…Anyone Home? *I wanted to let readers know where this information was coming from, so I asked my guides to introduce themselves. I've included that information here and have also added some information on specific guides and teachers who would be working on this particular subject matter—the crossing of a child. Here is their introduction.*

"First, we would like to introduce ourselves. We are a group of guides, teachers, and loved ones who have been working with Joseph throughout the years. He has shown an ability to interact with our side and to be able to transcribe our thoughts and messages. We have worked with him both physically and spiritually throughout his life. We have guided him through the ups and downs of his existence, and we have been directly involved in many cases of supporting him as to a particular direction he has chosen. He and only he has made the decisions and chosen the directions in his life. We have been there to support, guide, and love him throughout all his learning situations. Some would have you think that we are just various energies and consciousness flowing in and around his structure, but we are more than that. We are conscious beings who have made it our purpose to intercede and help guide individuals on the physical plane.

"Joseph was introduced to us as part of his courtship process of being chosen for the particular path that he entered into. From an early age, he was aware that we were interacting with him, and we continued to support him, even when he did not acknowledge our existence.

We have noticed an intense change in the energies surrounding Joseph, which enable us to tap into him more easily and with more confidence. He has shown a great disregard for the fear that is associated around this process. Also, he has agreed to work with us on a daily basis in order for us to train and help him to develop his mediumistic skills. We asked Joseph to communicate this particular knowledge, as we have seen a great need for it from individuals on your side and from individuals who have passed to our side. The interaction between the two sides has been vast at times, and we wish to make it more accessible to everyone who wishes to open their heart and think of the possibilities that they can achieve just by knowing that we exist."

I believe that a main group organizes these transfers of knowledge and that specific guides focus on different subjects. In my veterans book, Always Connected: For Veterans, *I noticed there were many veterans in the group who help bring that particular information to me. So I wasn't surprised to see that some of the guides who had been on the Earth plan at one time and had lost a child would be working on this book.*

For this new book, here are the guides who focused on this particular project concerning the loss of a child.

Joe, we are a group of entities who have visited your plane of existence in the past. Some of us have been to your existence multiple times and have experienced some of the things you will talk about in this book. Some have had children who have passed earlier than their expectations, while others have interacted with your side in dealing with such experiences and other trauma. We all work as a team on this particular project, as it has many different complexities to it. We also have advisors and guides to help us explain to you how the interactions between your plane and our plane are understood.

The children giving their insights have spent time on your physical plane and offer up this information in hopes of relieving the pain and suffering that they are witnessing on an ongoing basis. They see what their parents and loved ones are going through on a daily basis and wish to inform them that there is more to the picture than what they can understand. They have decided to group together and talk about certain particular subjects concerning their passing. They hope that some of their insights will help those who are currently struggling with the loss of a child. They also wish for this information to be made public so that others who may not have experienced the loss of a child will understand the process that parents and others who have lost a love one go through.

Together we work with a team of organizers and strategists. Their job is to organize the information in a way that your readers would most likely be able to understand. We realize that some of the information is complex, and Joe has requested that this information be brought through in an understandable manner. We wish to make sure that these concepts and experiences are able to be understood by different sections of society. By this, we mean adults and children in any culture or society.

As with the other books Joe has written, we pick a spokesperson who will transfer this knowledge so that he can put it into book form and other media through which people can access the information.

It's our honor to be working with this method of bringing this information from our side to your side in order to relieve the pain and suffering of so many. Many guides and teachers volunteer their focus and energy to help in this process. It is wonderful to have such a loving and caring team to work with to share this information, as we know it is much needed.

It is important for you to understand the reasons we wish to have this information transcribed. We hope that in the future you continue to listen and learn, as we will bring forth new information on other subjects that people wish to have advice on.

In this book, we want to focus on the surrounding complexities of losing a child.

As guides, we also oversee the transition of entering into human form and leaving that form to return back to your natural spiritual state. We can intercede to a certain extent, and we can bring comfort, support, and knowledge to those in human form. At times, we are asked to provide insight and creativity so that the human spirit can grow and appreciate the physical form that has been taken. Many times we instill ideas and concepts that human beings can take in and play out as they see fit.

This can be shown in the fields of healing, general health, and creativity, such as music, the arts, and a plethora of other areas of influence. We take our responsibilities with the utmost regard for your insight, safety, and growth.

Some of us have specific jobs in working with each individual. Some will focus on the human body, while others will work with the spiritual aspect. Some will work with emotional levels and balances, and others will work with creativity, insight, and ideas.

Not all your guides will focus on the individual. Some will focus on the opportunities that are available to each person. These guides work on organizing different groups that will interact in order for learning to take place. They help individuals come together in a group to share lessons and learning opportunities. They are tasked with setting up possible opportunities and allowing each individual to make their own decision if they wish to participate in it. Many of you know this as free will. It's our job to set the scene, and it is your decision to act on it, depending on which opportunities you decide to take and explore. So the many guides have different responsibilities and tasks, depending on each individual's goals.

Why This Subject

For now, we will focus on this one particular project—to help those who have lost children or who believe that the physical loss of their child is permanent and cannot be looked at in any other way.

The ultimate purpose of supplying this knowledge is to bring ease and relieve discomfort for those who have experience the loss of a loved one. When we say "child," in actuality it is any soul who has departed the physical plane before its path of knowledge has been entirely developed. Some leave too suddenly, some leave when they're supposed to, and others leave as a result of their own decision.

We will discuss all of these in much detail, some of those who have experienced it will be able to understand the different concepts related to crossing over when it comes to a younger person or the son or daughter of a parent.

We also want to transfer knowledge that will help others understand the process of how things work when it comes to experiencing trauma in their lives. Some may not have experienced the loss of a child but may have experienced trauma in other ways that need to be dealt with. We will focus a part of the book on this topic.

We understand that the subject of healing will be a section of this book and that people will have access to some insights in order to relieve the intense emotional pain they experience with these types of events.

What we wish to achieve with this book is to transfer the knowledge that's needed to understand the concept of a child when your sense of being is a young spirit. You view a child as someone new to the world with many possibilities for achievements, growth, and learning.

What we wish to do in this book is for adults and others who have reached certain stages of maturity to understand the concept of a child passing before they have reached certain milestones in their life.

We will not limit an age of the child who passes to an infant or toddler. For even adults who have gained vast knowledge and experiences can and are considered children to their parents and many other older adults who have had interactions with, and influence on, them. In the mind of the parent or family member, the younger person, no matter their age, is still a child to them as they remember the birth and experiences in the younger years of their existence. The bond was created through youth, and upbringing continues throughout the life cycle of all involved.

The passing of a child in the later years of its development may be not as profound as the passing of a child in its early stages of existence. However, it is the same concept of losing someone whose connection with others bridges many experiences.

Part of the reason for this book is to bring awareness to adults that there is more in play than the growth of an individual throughout their life. As adults interact with each other and create experiences, so do the children. A child's passing at the earlier stage of its development can have a profound effect on adults they come in contact with. These effects can be extremely positive, confusing, or even misunderstood. People need to know that there are other factors at play with the passing of the child.

It is difficult to tell a parent that their child was born in order to pass tragically or at an early age. This concept is very difficult to understand and appreciate. Not only will the parent or adult misunderstand this statement, but they will also tend to dismiss it, as they're unable to conceive that the child would plan their own passing while they had the ability to continue on and experience all the joys and happiness that a full life can afford.

Certain concepts will be explained to you in order for you to understand the process that is at play. However, many of these concepts and explanations will not be understood to the extent that we would like. We understand that once you reach a certain age of development, your ability to understand certain concepts becomes much harder.

But we must try to keep this information included, as some of it will resonate with certain individuals and cause others to rethink their own existence.

It is our expectation to help relieve the suffering and sadness that surround the death of a child. We will use certain concepts to explain this process as easily as possible. However, some of these explanations will not be understood because of the complexities.

We hope that some of these concepts that we explain are welcomed with the belief that a child is more than a child and that their existence has played out as it should have in that particular situation.

We will be talking about the ability of an individual to make their own choices and the ability of the individual to live their life free of obligations to their soul. However, certain determining factors must be taken into account when we discuss the passing of a younger child as opposed to the death of an adult.

In these instances, we can bring insights and so-called reason to the available topics in order for people to understand the possible outcomes and reasons things have happened.

The Process

The explanation of the process and transfer of knowledge was best described by my guides in my book Always Connected for Veterans. *It still stands true for the transfer of information concerning the passing of a child.*

"We seek out mediums and channelers in order to transfer information to your plane of existence. We need you to help us transfer this knowledge. We have other methods of interacting with your side, but at times it is easier to work through an individual, and so Joe has been chosen to be a part of this transfer of knowledge. When more detailed information and knowledge need to be transferred, we accept the fact that an individual is at times the best medium or way to accomplish this goal.

"The transfer of knowledge has been going on since the beginning of time. We work with individuals one-on-one but also work on larger subjects concerning many people, societies, and cultures. When people ask us questions, we try to give them legitimate answers. Information is not always allowed to be transferred due to the circumstances around the releasing of that knowledge.

"If all information were released to you on your plane of existence, many of the lessons that you came here for would not be able to be accomplished. You would have understood the concept of this information, but you would not have had the ability to experience it firsthand. It is one thing to learn something by the transfer of knowledge from one to another, and another thing to learn through experience.

"Some may say the holding back of this knowledge is wrong and that to do so causes much pain and suffering. This is not the reason this information is kept back. Your existence is specifically connected to experience things firsthand. Your potential growth would be stunted if this information were just handed to you. You see, the ultimate goal is to achieve this knowledge through firsthand experience and to be able to learn from it and grow at a spiritual level.

"'Then why is this information allowed to come through?' you may ask. Because at times this information is needed in order to understand the experiences that you are living. Often these experiences are of such magnitude that they can corrupt the learning and understanding of the experience. This can also corrupt the learning experience to the degree that the person's existence is not in line with the growth that has taken place. An example is if someone's experience is so traumatic that their ability to understand is compromised and new learning is stopped. Many may not understand this concept, but it is important to remember that just because you have the knowledge does not mean you have the understanding.

"So at times throughout history, we have contacted a few who have the ability to transfer this knowledge to the masses. We have the ability to do it on an individual basis, such as through creativity and prayer, in order to help them understand the meaning of life. At other times, we enjoy bringing through explanations and understanding of how the process of life works. There are concepts and explanations that will never be received in the way they are meant, and therefore they are held back. Once you are reunited on the spiritual side of existence, you will understand this concept.

"Some may be afraid to accept this information, while others may consider it to be false. Those who wish to downplay this information have a concern that it may come from a source that is not of the highest moral and ethical makeup. This is understandable, as information has been transferred from other entities that are not looking out for the best of humanity. They may wish to cause chaos and suffering through misinformation and the corruption of the process for their own personal, selfish, and ignorant reasons. They also may wish to pass on information that will serve their own purposes in order to gain strength on your plane of existence. We understand that many people have different names for these types of entities and interactions. But they all have certain things in common. They bring uncertainty; they bring harm, misunderstanding, and fear. These are signs that the information coming through is not necessarily from a higher order of existence.

"However, many times the information that comes through is from a higher order of existence, and it is meant to help humanity understand the experiences they are learning at this time. Those who fear this information are apt to have to recreate experiences over and over through many lives before accepting the knowledge that was presented to them at a previous time. An example of this may be a person learning how to swim. When they go near the water, they will touch the water, and then they will go in up to their knees and then come out. This can go on for years, as opposed to the person who will learn how to swim in just one summer. Others may not accept this information due to the fact that they are still trying to comprehend other information that has been passed along to them. This early information has not been fully analyzed and understood at a soul level, and they are not prepared to accept this new information on top of it. They become conflicted by accepting some information and not other pieces, and once you start to break up this knowledge in that particular way, it can become confusing and unreliable.

"So, our goal is to bring this information to as many people as possible and let each individual make their own choice as to the level of acceptance they are willing to take in order to use this knowledge to grow and understand this spiritual path.

"This knowledge we seek to pass over to you will cover many subjects and experiences in a human's life experiences. Some may be personal and spiritual, while other knowledge may be about how societies have developed and the particulars of the makeup and abilities of humans and the structures they lived within. Some may understand this under the term *science.*

"We understand that there are many cultural and religious differences between souls on the Earth plane. We are not going to discuss that in great depth in this book because we believe that information will take away the attention that needs to be focused on the subject we are discussing.

"If all people in all cultures were at the same level of development, it would be very difficult for individuals to move along the spiritual path and grow without having firsthand opportunities presented to them. Yes, there is a duality to life on the Earth plane. Some explain it that you cannot have good without evil, you cannot have compassion without suffering, you cannot have insight without ignorance. This is true to a certain extent; it gives you a scale or a base in order to see where you are in the learning process.

"Once you have crossed over and back to your original spiritual essence, you will see the experiences that you have lived with a different perspective. You will see the part that you played in your own development as well as the part you played in the development of others. Some may be limited to individual participation between souls, while others participation might be on a larger scale dealing with millions of souls at the same time. No matter which, your interaction with others will be the source of your learning and knowledge.

"We ask that this information that is coming through be used for the peaceful transition of the human experience and to bring about an awareness of the process of growth. We wish people to understand that our interaction with your side is brought about as a natural process of guiding humans on their path. It's like a parent guiding a child in learning new experiences.

"You are individual souls who are on a journey to increase your knowledge of life. By increasing this knowledge and understanding this information, a soul can progress to a higher state of enlightenment. As more experiences are learned and more information is assumed, your ability to pass on this information to others will be allowed. So, you are not only growing for yourself; you are growing in order to help others. You are all learning to become teachers, but you must first pass the courses of life on the Earth plane."

Section II

The Bigger Picture

"This is the concept of free will—the ability to change one's direction while living on the Earth plane..."

J.M.Higgins

Who Is A Child

A child is connected biologically to relatives as well as sharing some similarities, such as appearance and personality, with others who may now be adults. This association makes it difficult when the child passes over because those types of connections don't allow the real essence of the child to be recognized.

As the physical connection is broken between the child and their mother, father, siblings, and others who assist in the child's upbringing, those people will most likely process their feelings of loss based on that relationship and may not realize that the child is actually a fully independent spiritual being.

Even your society and various cultures will have similar feelings toward children, perceiving them as innocent, unknowing, unfolding non-adults. Society wishes to protect children, thinking there are horrible outside dangers and influences that may corrupt children's growth. To a certain extent, this is very true, especially on the Earth plane, where it has been designed that protection is needed in the early years of a being's life. The human species is very vulnerable at birth due to its inability to reason or to facilitate its own development in a quick and efficient way.

This is one of the reasons that the bonding of children with others is necessary—for growth within a protective environment. Children rely upon others to sustain their life during the early years of their development.

As children begin to grow and learn, they take on more responsibilities and begin to see themselves as individual beings in their own right. The associations and interactions between children and others are vitally important in their development. Without these interactions, children will not be able to develop, either physically or mentally, and will not have the strength to continue to be a presence on the Earth plane. At times, children can survive on their own to certain extent, but this is limited to special situations. With the advancement of medical knowledge and assistance in nurturing, the young children of the future will have more options in their early years to confront the obstacles that children face today.

When a mother gives birth to a child, it is a physical act that is experienced by the mother and also witnessed by others who may be present during this time. The physical act is very visual and exciting for all involved. There is great joy, and at times much sorrow, depending on the circumstances of the birth.

These are the physical attributes that surround the birth of the child. The complexities of the interactions between adults and the child are similar for all who experience them. The event is a combination of emotion, physical exertion, and the understanding that the life that has been created has the potential to become whatever it wishes.

The adults who witness the birth of a child will not always have the same expectations that others may put on the child at a later date. When a child is born, the expectations are very simple: a healthy baby breathing normally and able to function physically. These are all the expectations that are needed at the beginning of a child's life. After this initial stage, plans are made, expectations grow, and experiences are taken on from those surrounding the child. The experiences of adults can be absorbed by the child and can begin to skew the child's perception of the world.

We have not even discussed the child as an individual spirit soul because everyone assumes the child is immature in its physical as well as its mental and emotional state, and to a certain degree this is true. However, this child is the same spiritual being it will be at the apex of its life. Its expectations, experiences, and thought process might change throughout a particular time span, but the essence of who it is will not change. It will be the same at birth as when it is time to pass.

Many adults are unable to understand this concept. They see a defenseless young being who has no knowledge of the world and who cannot provide for itself as helpless. However, this child comes with a vast array of information and abilities. Some of these abilities may be dormant at the beginning of its life but will eventually come more out in the open as the child begins to age. These abilities can at times be changed by the environment the child is raised in. An example of this is a child who is brought up in a loving environment and a child who has been abused from a very young age and who concentrates more on personal survival, both physically and mentally, and thus does not have the ability to tap into some of its natural tools to help itself grow.

It is important for people to realize that certain children are born to carry out certain obligations and experiences, not only for their own benefit but also for the benefit of others who interact with them.

Some babies are welcomed into this world with open arms and are only expected to be simple, little, beautiful beings. While this may be true, they are also complex individual souls who will have an effect on others throughout their life, regardless of the duration of their lives or the environment they live in.

Children may be perceived as unknowing, but they have a vast array of tools that help them learn and grow at a specific rate. Some of these tools are used for a brief time in order for them to achieve certain levels of growth. Other tools and abilities will be used further on down the line of their life to help them and give them insight into the world in which they will live.

As adults, you have certain abilities that you can tap into and use in your everyday life, such as laughter, self-healing, past experiences, and knowledge. Children have all these concepts and tools when they arrive on the Earth plane—they have just not been activated yet. As a child develops, some of these attributes, such as intuition and the ability to feel others' energy, including love and fear, will open up and be used. As more time goes on and their interactions become more complex, these basic attributes that they came into this world with sometimes get twisted from their original meaning and misunderstood.

For example, certain children are more sensitive to outside stimuli than others. This ability may have been brought with them in order to experience certain things as they grow older. However, outside influences such as parents, siblings, coworkers, friends, and extended family may interact with these children and numb this ability to the point where it is not of use to these children and becomes dormant.

Oftentimes we see children who are quite aware of their surroundings as they soak in as much knowledge of this world as they can. However, as they associate with adults, they take on some of the adults' aversions, which can shut down some of their attunement to the life around them.

With some children, certain abilities may lie dormant for many years and resurface later in life. We see this with children who have shown no aptitude for music, art, or other creative forces that emerge later in life, to their wonderment, and are utilized to bring joy to themselves as well as others. The point is that they came into this world with abilities that, for one reason or another, lay dormant until later stages in life.

Not all children utilize all their gifts; they may utilize only a few in order to learn and experience what they came here to be exposed to.

While parents and other adults look at a child with the expectation of a full life of experiences, that is not always the plan when the child is born.

Children have a special place, and they have the ability to see life as it truly is: unfiltered. They have no preconceived opinions about cultures, people, or the realities of the world. They really are the purest form of humanity. They are open and trusting, with joyful love.

This is a brief explanation of the differences between adults' expectations and awareness of children at birth and the abilities and sense of children from their own perspective.

Why They Left

The general answer to the question of why children pass over is that, in your life experience, a transition is constantly occurring between spirit and human form. Life begins in physical form when a child is born on the Earth plane. When that spirit leaves its physical body to return to its natural form, it's considered death. This transition is a natural part of the human experience. It happens to all those who seek the knowledge and spiritual awakening available on the Earth plane and who have decided to take on the task of the physical form. Others may wish to take this path but are uncertain and do not step into the human experience. They will observe the ongoing growth of the spirits who fully join the human form.

Sometimes when children pass over at a young age, they have completed many tasks they came to be part of. Some will excel as the main character in a scene, while others will play backup roles that are as important to other individuals as they are to themselves. As opportunities play out, different results come into play. Some of these results will cause the passing of an individual before they have had time to complete other opportunities that have been arranged. This does not hurt their spiritual development—it only shortens the opportunities that are available.

When an individual decides to interact with other individuals in order to learn and grow, there are always different exits that are present. This means that the soul may take the opportunity to cross back over before they have completed other opportunities that would otherwise be available in the future. They are allowed to come back because they have fulfilled a majority of the things they had set out to accomplish.

Many times throughout an individual's life, they will have opportunities to leave the physical plane earlier than they had planned. This creates learning opportunities and understandings for others who are left behind. So, for an individual who decides to leave early by using one of these exit points, they are actually creating opportunities for the others who are left behind. This in itself creates spiritual growth for the individual who leaves. So, the person who leaves creates this learning opportunity from the fact that they have decided to leave earlier than had been planned.

Children pass over for a variety of reasons. Most importantly, most or all of their lessons have been completed. By crossing over, they are creating opportunities for learning for those left behind. This is immensely important to the growth of those who are left behind. That is why we see such grief and interruption of one's life after the passing of a child. It creates a larger opportunity for growth than other means that are available.

There is no right way or wrong way while going through the grief process. It's all learning. When a child leaves sooner than everyone expected, they are actually instigating the growth potential for all the others left behind. So not only have they accomplished many of their goals, but in leaving they also create the opportunity for major growth for those left behind. This unselfish act is created through the ultimate love between the individuals left behind and the spirit who has crossed over.

It can be difficult to accept this concept but on the spiritual growth level it's immensely important.

Children often cross due to circumstances outside their control. They may have interacted with other individuals or groups that caused the passing. Individual free will can create a complex structure of interactions. When a soul sees an opportunity for growth and interaction, they may decide at that point in their life to take advantage of the opportunity. However, this opportunity can also create an unbalanced situation for them and others at the same time. An example of this may be deciding to go with friends to a particular location at a particular time and being involved in a fatal automobile accident.

This is not to say that every fatal accident is caused by free will or someone taking the opportunity to join possible different outcomes.

Some accidents are early exits, others are preplanned, and still others are caused by free will. *In some instances, it is a combination of all three.*

Joe, you have an expression, "thinking on the go" or "winging it." This is an example of how some of the combinations may play out. If the spirit has a preplanned exit and others interacting with that spirit also see an opportunity for an early exit, they may decide to pass over at that time. Others, through free will, might put themselves in a position where an early exit opens up to them and they decide to take it.

So, the interactions can be quite complex, and the reasons for crossing over vary, depending on each individual spirit.

So, when someone asked the question "Why?" we want them to know there are multiple answers. Some are as simple as "It was their time." Others are as complex as interaction between multiple groups, with opportunities opening up on the fly.

It's important to remember that the "why" does not necessarily have to be answered. Many wish to know the exact reason, and with some investigation you may come to a conclusion that fits that individual. For example, so-and-so was an adventurer who lived his life to the fullest and wasn't afraid to take chances. Or someone's child was an "old soul" who acquired wisdom well before they had reached an older age and thus only needed to complete a few tasks in their lifetime.

We know you will always question why, but we also want you to know there truly is a reason for the way things play out. Even random acts that create a transition are choreographed to some degree by individuals, groups, and the person who passed.

We can touch base on this again but we do not want to make it overcomplicated to the point where you get too confused and nothing becomes understandable.

Soul, Life Plans & Free Will

※※※

The soul's objectives are planned out before birth with groups of other souls in order for certain learning experiences to take place. The soul plan will include certain achievements and opportunities that the soul wishes to accomplish while incarnate.

Can plans that are made before you arrive be altered once you begin the human experience? The simple answer is yes. This is what we call one's life plan.

A life plan is similar to a soul plan, as it is initiated before you arrive on the Earth plane. When a decision is made for you to accept the journey that you have chosen, your body is created, and the plans you have initiated begin to play out.

As you grow and achieve certain milestones in your soul plan, opportunities to learn different lessons will appear during your lifetime. The ability to interact in these new opportunities will be associated with the term *life plan*. The term *free will* has been used to describe the ability to interact, or change the course of one's life plan. This is true, to a certain extent, but is actually more complex than that.

In the life plan, an individual soul may choose to use its free will to make a decision involving a potential learning experience as it sees fit. By this, we mean you alone may choose the path to take, depending on the variables that your human body is awakened to. You may choose to accept a certain activity, depending on how your human reaction is integrated.

An example of this is a soul plan that includes the objective to save another person's life from drowning during the early part of one's life. The life plan may say you will be born in England and become a sailor in your midtwenties. However, after being born and raised in England, you choose to move to California and become a surfer in your twenties. The opportunity to save a drowning person is still intact for the soul plan, but the location and manner have changed the life plan through your free will.

The life plan is more fluid and involves more of a free will decision-making objective. The soul plan cannot be overridden by a life plan.

Many times these two levels of organizational planning can be confused and can cause distress. People will debate whether certain actions that have taken place were preplanned, and if so, why they would cause so much trauma to the individuals associated with a particular event.

Oftentimes these particular events are experienced as the soul having seen opportunities for growth and having chosen to interact with these situations as they arose.

This concept can be more easily explained as "learn as you go." You have the opportunity to fully integrate with your environment and create certain opportunities for growth that are within the general soul plan. The individual may pick and choose which learning experiences it wishes to become involved in. Oftentimes when a soul sees an opportunity for growth and decides to interact with that opportunity, it will in essence create a new experience for all the souls experiencing the event.

By this, we mean that if an individual decides to join a group for a particular reason, and if the events to be played out are part of the soul plans of the other participants, then this individual has decided to join in the entire group's lesson.

A simple example would be a person who decides to join a group of friends in a particular activity that causes the soul to transition back to our plane of existence. It may seem as if this sudden, tragic event has no meaning. But in essence, it is playing out as it had been planned. The soul who decided to join this learning opportunity becomes part of the group and therefore part of the outcome of this experience.

People often refer to this as being "in the wrong place at the wrong time." This is not true. It's actually being in the right place, as they have chosen at the right time for the others' learning experience. The individual has just accepted the opportunity to join the others in their experience.

Before the individual came to the Earth plane, this particular event would not have been preplanned. However, in the soul plan, the opportunity to learn from such an incident would be *available* to be played out at some time, in some place, within the individual's lifetime.

So some experiences that may seem uncalled for are being carried out at a different time and place than the original plan but under similar circumstances.

The soul plan is the overall set of opportunities that will become available during one's lifetime. There may be some specific instances that are to take place in order for that soul to grow. But overall, the soul plan will include multiple opportunities for growth experiences throughout the individual's life. These opportunities may be grouped into different categories, for example, health issues, relationship issues, and situational growth experiences. By situational growth experiences, we mean that opportunities are available for growth during different phases of the human experience, such as infancy, adolescence, adulthood, and the senior years.

By making available the situational opportunities, the soul can use its free will to decide when and how these situations will play out. For example, someone may have a health issue that will need to be played out in order for others surrounding them to learn a particular lesson. We see this when an illness brings a family together, creates compassion from caregivers, and brings new perspective about mortality to others.

Other times, that health issue may not be needed in order to bring similar lessons to those involved. The individual soul may take an opportunity that has arisen during adolescence to create a similar circumstances with those around them so they can achieve the same learning lessons but in a different manner.

Time, Perspective & Access Points

❦

We realize that this concept is very broad to begin with, but we will break it up into multiple areas so that those who need to know about specific parts of it will have access to the information that pertains to them.

In understanding the loss of a child, it needs to be understood that the connection between our plane and yours is in full motion throughout the duration of your life span.

If your belief is that life has a beginning, middle, and end, you are locked into a position or perspective in which you are limiting your ability to understand the process we call life.

You see, once you understand the vast aspects of how life works, you are better able to understand the process of losing a loved one and continuing on your own path while still on the Earth plane.

So, it is important that we start at the beginning and help you understand that the process of life is a continuation — it does not start when you're born on the Earth plane. It has begun many lengths of time before that. We will try to help you understand using your perspective of time. In actuality, time is an illusion; it has only been put in place to judge different aspects of one's growth and cycle of life. Many use time as a basis for creating and understanding change. Otherwise, life would be a continuous growing experience—which, in fact, it is.

When you choose to take your place on the Earth plane of existence, you have accepted the facts that go with that materialistic dimension. Some of the facts that are of concern to you are immaterial to us. These include the day/night manifestation, the wanting of objects, and the arguing over different interpretations of various questionable subjects.

We are more concerned about the growth of the individual as well as groups of souls that make up various countries, cultures, and nations that you're aware of. Sometimes our influence can be seen when it is converged into a particular group that makes its ideas known to the larger population. You will see this when groups organize for various charity events or to bring awareness to vital subjects affecting everyone on the Earth plane.

But for now we will focus on losing a loved one from your plane of existence and returning back to their original area of influence in our dimension.

When people begin to understand the concept of birth and death, they realize that they're concerned about the length of this term. Many people actually celebrate each year that has passed and congratulate each other on this milestone. In actuality, this is a cultural phenomenon and does not help in the knowledge of the true aspect of life and death.

When life begins on your plane of existence, there are various degrees, or avenues, that an individual will be able to access throughout their life. These access points are very important, as they are the times and experiences when certain influences will come into their life in order for them to grow and experience the necessary knowledge they are seeking.

So, it is not the length of time in an individual's life that determines the person's path; rather, it's the quality of life and experiences that have been planned out that must be taken into consideration.

While some believe that certain tragedies can cut short a person's life and deny them the experiences and love they would have been involved in if they had continued to live on your plane of existence, in actuality some of these tragic events occur as a situation plays out in order for the individual to learn and grow from such situations.

An individual may be involved in such a situation as the primary member who has gone ahead of others to enable the others to learn and grow from their experience. At other times, an individual may be an observer and may witness an event to learn and grow and experience the outcome of that particular event for their own growth.

So there are multiple players in each situation, and the particular part your love one plays will determine the lessons and knowledge that are learned or that have the potential to be learned.

An example of this is the sudden death of a loved one in a car accident that also has survivors. Family members and other loved ones will question why one person died and not another. In this particular situation, the person who died was in fact the leader of this event on a spiritual level. This individual was willing to accept this access point in order for others on larger scale to grow and learn from the situation.

In times like these, the words *tragic* and *wasteful* often come into play. We wish to change this perspective. As with many of these types of events, they are actually growing experiences that can only be achieved through that particular situation. It is difficult for many people to understand this concept, but it is vitally important that they try to learn the reason behind it.

One's perspective has to be able to shift in order to understand these concepts. Otherwise, they will create more questions and may also create a lack of ease with the satisfaction of a particular answer. We will try to explain the process so it is as understandable as possible.

Not all tragic events occur because of the playing out of the particular situation in order for spiritual growth to all involved. Some events occur due to other situations that are playing out with other groups of individuals, and when we say groups of individuals, we mean groups of souls.

Some of these events will take place on a larger scale and will interact with other events that are occurring at the same time for different reasons. This can be complicated to explain, but think of a circle partially overlapping another circle within a third circle. The interactions of many groups and individuals are happening at the same time; some overlap for a particular purpose while others become involved in the other situations by virtue of a changing learning experience plan.

Many of you realize that you have free will to act in experiencing life to a certain degree. Some people stay directly on their life's path from the moment they are born to the moment they transition back to where they started. Others take a more roundabout route, crossing over between other living experiences and searching for new experiences that were not originally planned out before they arrived here. This is the concept of free will—the ability to change one's direction while living on the Earth plane while still completing the lessons and acquiring the knowledge needed for the soul's growth and understanding of the higher concepts of love and compassion.

So, while many will be going from point A to point B, some will be making side stops in many different areas. When this happens, they may be subject to the experiences that are happening to other souls at that particular time. What one may believe to be "wrong place, wrong time" could, in actuality, be the right place at the right time. Things will play out as they might have, but just in a different place and situation. An example of this is someone who is riding in a car that is in an accident and is killed while they were experiencing a sidebar, if you will, of their life's path. It may in actuality be an experience that was meant to play out at a different place and time. It could have been *before* or *after* this particular tragic event.

For others for whom it may not have been their time, enough lessons and experience have accumulated by then for them to be part of this experience yet create new situations and possibilities for their loved ones on the Earth plane.

The interactions between individuals, soul groups, and national souls are complex. An individual's direction on their path can change at any time during their life span. Their final destination and the completion of certain experiences are fixed before they come to the Earth plane. However, how they get to that final destination can involve many different routes, depending on which one the individual decides to take.

There are different levels of experience each individual soul will be asked to experience—by themselves as well as with colleagues and spiritual advisors before they come. Some will have a very short life span, and others will experience a great deal of time on the Earth plane, interacting with and affecting many individuals. The exact life plan is created on an individual basis, while the interaction of that life plan will also take into account the interactions with larger groups over time.

It is our understanding that you have a limited perspective on the concept of time; therefore, we are trying to put things into a perspective that you understand. You are taught from an early age that segments of your life are broken up into time periods: early development, adolescence, middle age, and the senior part of your life span. However, experiences can occur at any of these levels at any time. An infant can learn experiences and help in the growth of others in a very short period of time and can be just as influential and powerful as someone who has been on the Earth plane for many decades.

So, the main theme we have been trying to explain here is the *perspective of time*. When you look at a child, you think of the lack of life experiences and the unfulfilled possibilities ahead of them. When you look at a senior, you assume they look back at what they have experienced throughout their life and that certain experiences will no longer be available to them due to their age.

What we want you to understand is that both of these individuals have the ability to create experiences for anyone at any of their stages of life. When you think about a child learning to ride a bike or a senior having difficulty walking, we wish for you to understand that the experiences these two individuals are creating for the growth of others are the same. This is very important.

This is the concept we are trying to get across: **The age of the individual is not correlated with their ability to create experiences for growth and understanding of love and compassion.**

While looking at the child learning how to ride a bike and the senior struggling to walk, you're looking at the linear perspective of time rather than the important part of the spiritual growth of each individual's soul.

Once you begin to understand this concept, it will give greater meaning to your own life and to those around you as you interact with them.

Exit Points

~~~~

Souls can take advantage of certain "exit points" that are created before they comes to the Earth plane. These exit points are opportunities for the soul to return to its original environment at a preselected time. If a soul has achieved the majority of its lessons that it came here to experience, it may decide to return earlier than had been planned. The reason for this is that continuing to live on the Earth plane may bring additional pain and suffering to those who are close to the individual. For if the soul decides to remain, additional lessons will play out that might not be necessary. If the lesson has been learned by those who are meant to experience it, it is not necessary to play it out again in order to achieve its original result.

Sometimes people will misunderstand this concept and believe they have experienced multiple lessons that seem to be the same. They may ask why something is happening to them over and over again. In essence, it is because they have not experienced the lesson to its fullest extent. This may be difficult to understand from your perspective, and it is one of those situations where most people will not understand fully until they cross back over to the spirit realm.

Each soul is given several exit point opportunities to be used at the discretion of that individual soul. The decisions involve how different events will be used to decide if and when an exit point will be used. Oftentimes people ask why this had to happen now. And this is the reason: the individual has decided on a soul level to interrupt its length of life on the Earth plane because certain lessons have already been achieved, and lengthening its existence could cause others to abruptly change their soul plans and not be able to achieve the lessons they came to learn.

Author

I was shown how these exit plans work by a young girl name Karla. Karla's parents had sought me out for a mediumistic reading after the passing of their eleven-year-old daughter. We did the reading through Skype a few months after her passing. After initial contact with their daughter, it was determined that it was in fact their child. Karla has a wonderful personality, much older than her chronological age. She showed up wearing a pink boa, and I'm thinking, Is this really her? *The mother said Karla loved to wear a boa and throw it over her neck in a dramatic way. Also, her favorite color was pink. Kids usually come through pretty strong, and in Karla's case it was very true. The parents wanted to ask some questions, with the main one being "Was it someone's fault?" Now, my analytical brain thought that of course it had to be someone's fault because she was only eleven. So I asked Karla, and she responded, "No." Now my brain was back in gear, thinking,* How do I tell them no one was at fault, especially if she might have died in a car accident? I don't want to bring distress to them. *As a medium, you have to be aware of the people you are reading for and not bring them more suffering and pain. However, we also have to tell them what we are getting. So I turned off my analytical brain, which should be off during a reading anyway, and told them, "No, it was no one's fault." She said it was her decision to leave at that time. Then she showed me her long hair whipping forward over her head as if a sudden impact had cause her to flip over and caused her death. The parents then said she had died in an ATV accident. After using it all day, she wanted one last ride, and they forgot to put her helmet on. The guilt had not allowed them to sleep at all for weeks. After hearing Karla's explanation, the relief on their faces was instantaneous. They then asked about her decision to leave. That's when Karla showed me how exit points work.*

She showed me a highway with an exit ramp to my right and another exit ramp not too far up the road on the left. Then I was shown that the road continued, but not too far in the distance it abruptly stopped. I got the feeling her life was meant to be short. Karla said she took the first exit because it would bring less suffering for her and her family later on in life.

The parents said it made a lot of sense, as Karla suffered from a blood disease that would have left her bedridden in a few years, and she was not expected to live through her twenties. Thus, the highway was shown ending abruptly.

During many other readings with Karla and her parents, we all learned new things about exit points and various other reasons for an early departure. Karla was a driving force in my wanting to write this book so I could bring this information to other grieving people who had lost a child.

When an individual comes to the Earth plane, they do not come as an individual alone—they come with souls whom they will integrate with to learn, experience, and grow. Some souls will come before the individual arrives, while others will arrive after the individual has already begun its life lessons. So, the individual's life lessons and growth are also helping teach lessons and growth to others they come in contact with.

If one decides to alter their life's plan and interact with other souls that they had not originally planned on interacting with, they will take on a role that the other souls are playing out. Sometimes this role may be very similar to an original plan but just happens to take place under different circumstances.

When a Child Passes

After the death of the human body, the spirit encased in the soul leaves the human vessel and returns to its original place of being. By this, we mean that the soul returns to where it came from. Many people wonder if the soul transitions to a new location, and we would like to inform you that it returns to its original place of being. Some spirits will continue on into other growth opportunities, but when they first pass, they are reunited with their fellow souls in order to recuperate from their travels.

As the soul leaves the body, it recognizes, for the first time in many years, that it is separate from the confines of the body. A child, who may not have extensive experience with the human body, accepts this separation more easily when it occurs, for it has not had enough time to grow comfortable with the state of being confined in a human body. As an individual ages on the Earth plane, it becomes more difficult to recognize that they are not the body they are attached to. Through teachings, cultural influences, and self-awareness, individuals can become aware that they are more than their physical body.

The crossing child likely has a much easier transition, as it will often accept the new surroundings very quickly. An adult who transfers over may also accept its surroundings very quickly; however, at times an adult may need some extra comfort when they transition to make them aware that they have indeed crossed back into their original form of spirit.

Once the transition has occurred, the spirit is surrounded with love as well as understanding of the situation. There are those who are trained to greet the soul as it arrives in its new location. These so-called greeters may be loved ones who have been recognized from the Earth plane or others who have traveled with the soul on other adventures.

A child is welcomed home through a series of connections. These connections are actually transitional points from your plane of existence to ours. The time it takes for this transition to occur can be a matter of seconds or slightly longer, depending on the cause of the transformation. If a child had been ill for a longer period of time, the transition might take a little longer in the healing environment. This type of environment is surrounded with love and understanding. It gives the child time to adapt to the freeing feeling they now have. A child who had physical limitations for some time before passing and now does not have these limitations will learn to accept and become acclimated to their new freedom in this place of healing.

Some people have described this place of healing as similar to a hospital on your plane. However, this is not entirely true. The soul already knows it is free and full of love. It knows that healing has taken effect as soon as the transition has begun. This stage of the transition is more like a welcoming party that simply allows the soul to realize it's not part of the physical human body.

Once the child is acclimated to their new surroundings, they are free to move forward to greet those with whom they wish to interact.

This may include siblings, parents, or other close loved ones who have been on the Earth plane at the same time and now reside with them. The child also has the ability to begin to interact with individuals they have left behind. These interactions include the ability to share the idea that they have not died in the true sense of the word. The child will interact with others in the spirit world in order to facilitate a series of signs to send to loved ones who have been left behind.

These signs will be worked out in order for them to be accepted as easily and rapidly as possible. Many times the signs are not accepted due to the fact that the loved ones are not able to understand this new form of communication. The child will often want to contact parents and siblings as soon as possible. However, some will be in such grief that this is not possible, so attempts will be made at different times.

The child will be accepted with open arms, as they have played their part in creating situations and avenues for the growth of the souls they have left behind. Many times when a child passes, there is disruption among those who are left behind. It is part of the human experience to go through acute emotional and physical changes after the passing of a loved one. But when a child passes before those on the Earth plane feel it is time, it can cause greater discomfort among those left behind.

The child understands this when passing over and will try to communicate to those left behind that this soul actually continues after the transition called death. There may be great sorrow concerning the passing, and this can block any attempt to bring a sign through. Other avenues will be used, if possible, to transfer this information, such as through friends, colleagues, and other loved ones.

While this transformation of the soul continues, it will continue to grow as a spiritual being. It will interact with others in the spirit realm as it did before coming to the Earth plane. The soul will not feel isolated or alone, as it knows that's never possible because it is always surrounded with love and friends. It accepts its new surroundings with ease and is ready to begin its new work on the other side.

Transitional Stories

Amy

Hi, I'm Amy. I was twelve years old when I passed. I didn't pass over too quickly—it took a little bit of time. I was sick for a while, and my mother took care of me. She took a lot of time off work so she could be with me. I know when I passed that she was very sad and would cry all the time. I could feel her sorrow from where I was.

I was going through a lot of changes at that time, as I was looking forward to learning how to drive, and I wanted to be like my sister. My sister was grown up, and she had the most beautiful brown hair down to her shoulders. She was tall, too. (Amy is now giggling.) I was looking forward to getting taller and being able to drive and be out with my friends. But I was too sick to be able to go to school. I tried to continue with my studies but got to the point where I couldn't concentrate, so I had to let them go. I did have friends who came by and talked to me, so that was good. I liked to sing with them, but I only could do that for a little bit of time toward the end.

I knew I was getting ready to pass over when I became really sick.

I know it sounds strange for someone my age to talk this way, but deep down I knew I was going to die. I wasn't feeling well, but my mom was strong and she held my hand. I let her talk to me as much she wanted to; it made me think about how special I was to her. She held me tight until I passed over.

And then I was standing there right beside her. She wasn't sure if I was still in my body, but I wasn't. I could feel her energy and what she was thinking. I remember she was exhausted from taking care of me. She said she was sorry for everything I had to go through. I knew it wasn't her fault—I knew she didn't have a choice, and I knew everything was supposed to happen the way it did.

Sometimes I think back to that time and how close we were, but other times I remember her wanting me to catch up with her. She wanted me to tell her everything that was going on in my life.

Mom was very sad when I passed, and I could feel it right away. She was emotionally broken, and physically she was a mess. I felt great because I didn't have any more pain and I was aware of everything. I could sense others around me, and I was happy to be where I was. Mom's energy was denser than I had understood when I was living. I can sense when people are lighthearted and when they are grieving now. The energy that people give off is really easy to read. I learned that right away after I left my body.

So, I just wanted to come by and explain my experience of my transition. I also want to let you know that it was easy to leave my body and be whole again. There are times when people struggle with this, but it's not necessary. It just happens like this (Amy snaps her fingers). So, I just wanted to let people know it's not difficult to leave the physical plane.

Jonathan

Hi, my name is Jonathan. I was in the sixth grade when I passed. I left my house early one morning, and my grandma was giving me a ride to school. I was in an accident, and it was pretty traumatic because it caused me to come over to this side.

I remember the moment it happened. We were going down the street, and a car came up beside us and hit the front of the car. My grandma was shocked, and I was thrown into the side of the door. I think they said my neck broke. My grandma was hurt very badly, too. She was taken to the hospital and had to be sedated in order to heal from her injuries. She had problems walking after that and needed to use a cane.

I knew I was dead because all of a sudden, the light was different where I was. Everything glowed from within. Things seem to be alive, and everything was really cool. Everything around me was comforting. I was like, *Wow, this is what happens when you die.* I wasn't in any pain at all. Actually, I was feeling very loved.

I could see what was going on at the accident scene, but I was also totally aware of what was happening to me where I was. A couple of friends I had known who had died previously came up to me and said hi. I smiled when I recognized them, and I was like, *Wow you guys are really here.*

There is a lot more about my transition that I could go into, but for now I just want to let you know that I didn't suffer and I met friends and I was aware of what was happening to others left behind. So I hope this helps some people who have lost children to see that they're not alone in some dark place and lost. Not at all—it's really wild where I am … so much love.

Bob

Hi, Joe. My name is Bob. I was from California, and I passed when I was twenty-seven.

It was early nighttime, and I was driving. She was sitting next to me when I was in a car accident that caused me to pass over. It's okay for me to talk about it because I know it'll help others realize what happens when something like this takes place.

I was out with my friends after work, and we were playing around in the car and not paying attention. We ran a stop sign and collided with another vehicle. Two people in my car transitioned, and one person in the other car also died. It was difficult at first because I was confused as to what was happening. I don't mean the trauma, but more about where I was. I could see what was going on at the accident scene, but I felt as though I was outside of my body. It's strange to see things from that perspective. Once I realized what had happened, I started to look around, and I noticed the others. We all looked at each other, realizing what had just happened. We didn't say anything to each other—we didn't have to because we could hear each other and what we were thinking.

We realized that everything happened so quickly, and our opportunity on the Earth plane was over. We knew there was more to it than what we were aware of. We knew that there was a bigger picture and that we all fit into it, but we didn't know the exact details at that moment.

There is a lot going on in a situation like that, and you try to figure out what's happening to your body, which isn't the same as the body in the car. But you realize it pretty quickly and you adjust almost instantly, actually. What you may think is a longer period of time for us was very quick.

We were greeted by a few people at the scene of the accident. They were already there waiting for us. They knew the transition was going to occur. We were surprised that that was our life exit—our "out"—and that we had decided to leave at the same time and that it was something we had agreed upon. We didn't know when it happened, but we realize that afterward. I didn't hold back my feelings when I passed. It was so easy to open up and see who we really are. It's not like on the physical plane, where you have to hide parts of yourself from others because you don't want to be judged or ridiculed. It was very freeing to be able to drop that coat, or covering, as you might say.

It's amazing how the whole transition works. You're just here, all of a sudden, and it's so freeing compared to the physical plane. I mean, a lot of things are similar here, but there's no emotional baggage—there's no complaining because everyone accepts you for who you are, which is really cool. It's hard being on your side—really hard. I don't miss it; I miss some of the people, but I'm still close to them, so it's not really as if I don't get to see them anymore. I know what they're up to, I know where they're headed, and I can see what's going to happen to them, to a certain extent. But like anything, plans change, and you guys can do that with your free will. In my case, it was pretty standard procedure of what was going to happen. We all just decided it would take place at that time and at that intersection.

So please don't blame anyone if it happens to someone you know. It might have been part of a bigger picture. That's why I wanted to come through and let you know my feelings. Thanks, Joe—I wish you great success with the book.

Crystal

Hi. My name is Crystal, and I was thirty-four when I crossed. I wanted to come through to tell you my experience. I had known for some time that I was getting ready to cross, and as the time got closer, I realized I wasn't fully ready to die. I put myself through a lot of turmoil and anxiety before I passed, but then realized it wasn't necessary. You don't need to be afraid of something that is totally natural, like walking from one room to another. I put myself through the works trying to understand the meaning of life and why I was born and now why I was to die. There was no reason that was good enough to accept at that time. I wanted a nice, simple answer, but that wouldn't happen. What helped me the most was realizing that I would see my grandparents again and that their love would be there waiting to greet me. This gave me so much comfort that I actually began to look forward to crossing over.

When it's your time to cross over, you have to realize that your perspective begins to shift. What was important in the past is no longer important. The drama you were caught up in is gone. It's simply a time to look back at your life and see if you were a good person. I didn't really care about my accomplishments—it was more about how I treated people. That was the main concern. I was happy with the way I had lived my life, and although I didn't want to die, I realized that there was something special waiting for me on the other side.

When I finally crossed over, I could see everything in a new light, meaning I could see why I made all the decisions I did and how they affected other people's lives. I could see how my interactions with individuals caused certain outcomes for the better and others for the worse. The worst ones really weren't that bad, as my intentions were not to hurt anyone; it just happened that sometimes I did hurt their feelings.

So you get to see how everything played out in your life—everyone you came in contact with, how you dealt with certain situations, and even how you learned to laugh and play and accept new experiences. It was really interesting to watch how I developed throughout my life by looking at my interactions with others.

My family was very close, and I was part of a group of friends who at times were even closer. By looking at the way the group interacted, I could see how certain lessons were playing out for each individual on the spirit level. I could see that there was a reason for everything and why certain situations played out the way they did. Some things you would never guess. It's funny because when you're alive over there, you think you've got everything figured out. You think you know where the chess pieces go, but most of the time you really don't. So what I'm trying to say is don't try to figure out where the pieces go—just live your life. Take some chances, treat everyone with respect, laugh with your friends, laugh at yourself, and enjoy the short time you have on that plane of existence. By the way, it's great over here. I don't want to leave … but just maybe (she says with a wink and a smile).

Sign Stories

Soul Group

A couple of weeks after my nineteen-year-old daughter died in a car accident on Route 44 in Taunton, MA, I heard the most amazing story from my brother. We were all still so shaken from the tragedy, and my brother was teary-eyed as he told me what was repeated to him by an acquaintance. The woman he talked to said, "I heard a story about your niece, but I don't want to upset you." My brother told her it was okay—that he wanted to hear it. This woman said that three teenagers from Rehoboth, MA, who were a couple of years behind Erin in high school had been driving on Route 44 in Rehoboth, several miles down the same road that Erin crashed on. It was a rainy night, and the male driver began to lose control and the car hydroplaned. The teens were spinning in the road and were sure they were going to crash into a tree, as it was a rural area. All of a sudden, the car stopped. It was off the road, but nothing was hit and they all were unharmed. When the police arrived, the male driver said to the cop, "I don't want to sound crazy, but right before the car stopped I saw Erin Noble. She was just standing there in a yellow dress, smiling."

The two girls told their parents the exact same story. As my brother told me this story, I said, "Jeff, you're not going to believe this, but I buried Erin in a yellow dress." Nobody knew this because due to the nature of the injuries, we had a closed casket. Erin was always helping people when she was here on Earth, and I truly believe she is still full of love and light and is watching over us and helping us.

Michele Pearce, mom of Erin Noble
(forever nineteen years old)

Author
What a wonderful validation that Erin was still involved in helping people. This sign was passed through a few people in order for it to reach her mom. By being shared, it becomes a stronger sign and affects the whole community as the possibility of an afterlife comes into the consciousness of each person hearing the story.

There is also a connection between those teenagers and Erin on a spiritual level, as she intervened in their event. The complex nature of our soul groups leads me to believe they all were connected on a higher level.

The Light

It will be one year on October 22 of this year that my son, Nicholas Thau, graduated from this life. I have a wonderful story that I would be proud to have in your book.

About six years ago, I purchased a small light called "the Wave." I purchased it for Nicholas for his birthday. Nicholas had been confined to a wheelchair since shortly after birth. He was unable to use his arms or legs and had very limited neck control. He adored lights, fireworks—anything that lit up. So I purchased this "Wave" and put it on his nightstand. It made different-colored moving waves on his ceiling. HE WAS IN LOVE WITH IT. Every night it went on, and he would fall asleep to it. We took it everywhere with us—our three Disney cruises, Grandma's, hotels, and especially when he was hospitalized, which was often. For six years we didn't miss a night to turn it on. It was so soothing for him.

When he graduated (passed away) in October 2016, I kept his room exactly as it had been. I had forgotten about the little white box that made such beautiful multicolored moving waves. I was just used to it being there on the table. One evening, my husband and I went to dinner. As we returned home, my nineteen-year-old son was just getting in at the same time we were. Just the three of us live in the house now. I went into Nick's room, as I always do, to say goodnight. I looked on his bed, and there was a round piece of plastic, smack dab in the middle of his bed. The room was only lit by the small night-light in the hall, so it was fairly dark in his room. I picked up the round plastic object and had no idea what it was. I asked my husband, and he didn't know either. We searched his room and figured out that it was the top of his little wave maker. We didn't even know the top came off! Christopher ran up the stairs, and I asked him if he had put it in the middle of Nick's bed. He said no, that he never went into Nick's room, plus he was at work all day. My husband was with me, so he didn't do it.

It had been three weeks since my son had left. We firmly believe that this was Nick's sign to let us know that we had forgotten to turn on the light for him at night. Since that time, my husband or I go into his room every night to turn it on.

In memory of Nicholas Michael Thau

Author

This is an example of how something of meaning can be used to show a sign. The light brought great joy to Nicholas as well as his parents. So, it would be the perfect object to gain their attention. And by lighting it afterward, they sent their own message saying the sign was accepted and loved.

The Moon

I had just gone to the Dominican Republic with my family. It was the third time I had been there since we left the island permanently in 2004. It was extremely bittersweet seeing how much had changed and how much was still there. Although I was extremely grateful to spend time with family I hadn't seen in years, I recall thinking how much I wished the family on the other side was still around to see as well. I reflected on my life while I lived there and how it was while they were still on Earth as well. I recall asking my grandpa, whom I believe to be my guardian angel, as well as my sister Karla, for a sign that they were there, too. I released it. On our last night there, I was sure the experience had been enough, even with not getting a sign. Right as we got up to our hotel on our last night, I put my daughter down for the night and recall sitting by the window overlooking the Caribbean Sea. Just as I pondered my life as a little girl there, the brightest pink supermoon rose low above the ocean. I had never seen a moon so bright or so pink. My sister's nickname was Pinky. Right then and there, I had this feeling that all my family in spirit was around me.

In memory of Karla

Author

After asking for a sign and not initially receiving one, she determined that the vacation was still wonderful. By not putting a negative emotional attachments on a request, such as anger or disappointment, it allowed for the sign to occur naturally. Sometimes signs can be subtle, and at other times, like this one, they can be as big as the moon.

Finding Each Other

My son Zachary passed in 2006. A few months after my wife died in 2016, I was having a really hard time coping. My sixteen-year-old son was suicidal, and I was sitting at my table and felt a sudden draft. Then, all of a sudden, I could smell Zachary. I could always smell him from day one, and I knew his spirit was with me, watching over me. I knew then that I would get through this with his presence and guidance.

On another occasion—again, a very difficult day—I heard a bird calling. It was tweeting everywhere I went. My wife and I, when we were teenagers, would use that same call to find each other at places like the market because she was so short and hard to find in a crowd. I knew that day would be okay once I heard that tweeting.

In memory of Zachary Dauphinee

Author

Here is another great example of our loved ones trying to give us strength when we are having difficult days. Familiar things are important when giving and receiving a sign—in this case, his son's smell and a shared signal between his wife and him. Loved ones who have passed know what's going on in our lives. Remember to open you heart and receive this comfort. It will give you peace and strength in your time of need.

His Voice

Fourteen months after my son, Coby, was killed on his motorcycle by a reckless motorist, I was driving in my car and thinking about the cardinal ornament I had ordered to put on his memorial tree. It was planted in the neighborhood at the home where he grew up. It was on a small lake, and he loved the lake—he loved nature. A voice came in my head loud and clear, and I knew instantly it was Coby. The voice said, "Mom. I'm here with you" over and over, as if someone had left a bunch of messages on an answering machine and I had pressed "play." I was sobbing on my way to meet clients for work, and I had to pull myself together. I spent about three hours with them and then got in my car for the one-hour ride back to my home. Again I heard the voice; this time it said, "I'm okay, Mom" about four times. I believed I'd had "small" signs since his passing, but I doubted them and thought there was always an explanation. But this time I KNEW.

Only one other time in my life did I have that voice in my head... it was shortly after my dad passed away about six years ago. At about 3:30 in the morning, the voice in my head said, "Go look in the garage." I tried to ignore it because I didn't want to get out of bed, but it was persistent. So I got up, went downstairs, and opened the garage door. There was a strange light on in the garage. I was confused. I looked around, and there was an old night-light that had not worked in a decade but was still plugged into an outlet. I knew immediately that my dad had sent me a sign and thanked him. That light stayed on for two nights, then went off. I live alone, so there was no chance that anyone had touched it.

In honor of Coby Beaumont

Author

Coby found that the most successful way to get through to his mom was through a direct connection into her consciousness. Her dad had used the same technique to send a sign, so it's not unusual for the same method to be repeated if it's successful. Don't doubt the signs you receive—they're a gift. Thank them and enjoy knowing your loved one is still with you.

JOSEPH M. HIGGINS

Giving Blood

My son, Aymen, had a tattoo on his side in Italian. Translated, it said, "What we do in life echoes in eternity." I always wondered why he got that particular saying, but nevertheless we associate it with Aymen whenever we see the quote.

The other day I went to give blood. I don't usually give blood, but I have had many friends with children who transitioned because of cancer, so I thought I would donate. I told Aymen I was doing it in his honor to help all the people who needed it. I asked Aymen to send me a sign that he was with me and knew I was doing it for him.

When I arrived at the bloodmobile, they asked me which arm I use to give blood. I told them my right arm. But for some reason they told me to go to the back of the mobile unit to the left arm side. I sat down and was thinking about honoring Aymen and was looking out the window. I said in my mind, "Aymen, please give me a sign." I looked up and there was my sign right in front of me! "What we do in life echoes in eternity" was written on a whiteboard attached to the wall.

I never would have seen the sign if they would not have sent me to the back, even though they should have had me sit in the front with the "right arm" people.

In memory of Aymen Soussi
By his mother, Tracy Soussi

Author
This is a great example of how they can gain access to someone's consciousness in order to have that person say a particular thing—in this case, sending her to the back of the bloodmobile instead of up front, which would have been

the normal procedure. Aymen had directed her to that particular bloodmobile and influenced her seating. It is also probable that he had influenced the person to write that saying on that particular board.

Section III

Relationships

"Children have the ability to feel and sense at a higher level than most adults."

J.M.Higgins

Group Grief

When tragedy occurs, or even a simple passing that is expected, many emotions are being dealt with. Most of these are what you would call the primal emotions of anger, fear, anxiety, and even love.

The shock to the physical and mental system of the human body takes place on different levels, depending on the individual. Some people can accept certain circumstances more easily than others. This is not to judge or compare one person with another, as their makeup may differ and cause this reaction.

As many individuals interact during the transition of a child, there will be times when many points of contention will be made. By this, we mean that people experience grief in individual ways, and interacting with each other under these circumstances can cause conflict due to misunderstanding each other's makeup.

Oftentimes interactions between loved ones can bring back fond memories, laughter, and a closer bond between individuals who may have distanced from each other in the past. These are opportunities to balance your system and to help in accepting the passing. When love is introduced into the dynamics, it can create a systemic healing for all involved. Past discussions, actions, and feelings may be put aside as the more important issue of the child's passing takes center stage. These are times when people realize that life on the Earth plane is truly short and that being involved in conflict is not a good use of the limited time you have.

A child's passing can acutely reorient a group's dynamics. This may occur within an immediate family or among friends, colleagues, or even strangers. For all those concerned, it creates a new dynamic for growth.

A child sees this from the other side and tries to influence the group by surrounding it with loving energy to energize all involved. This can be seen when certain members of a family or friends who have not communicated in many years reestablish a loving connection. The child has assisted in this reconciliation.

Other times we see conflict break out, and this is strictly due to the imbalance individuals are experiencing in their current emotional and mental states. Certain individuals are unable to deal with certain events in their life and lash out. This is a physiological manifestation and does not always mean that there is hate in their heart.

In the relationship between a child and their family—and by this we mean the whole unit consisting of the biological parents or whoever raised the child as well as siblings—a dynamic will exist that needs to be addressed.

This dynamic is a melding of energies between all the participants. Their energies work together as each of them plays out the role they were willing to take on in this particular life. So, when one of them is involved in a traumatic situation, all of them will be affected.

The factions inside the family unit will deal with the passing of a child in various different ways, depending on each individual's makeup. Each person's experiences as well as physical and emotional makeup is often quite different from those of the others in the family.

It is important to understand that any child left behind will also know that things have changed in the dynamics of their own situation. The loss of a sibling is different from an adult losing a child. By this, we mean that an adult who has lost a child is often focused on the child who has passed.

The sibling who has lost a brother or sister or perhaps even a cousin or friend not only has to deal with the loss itself but also deal with a parent, relative or other caretaker who's dealing with the same loss.

However, there are more dynamics in parent-child relationships than in sibling-sibling relationships. And when we say parent-child, we include adults who are not biologically related who have lost a child they brought up, cared for, or were otherwise connected to.

Different people experience grief in many different ways. Adults have various ways of going through the grief process, and younger people also have various ways. Other relatives and people who were not as closely linked to the one who passed will grieve as well, and their feelings must also be taken into consideration.

Adults may often feel guilty that their focus is on the child who has passed and that their time is not being proportionally given to children who are left behind. But even in this situation, they may continue to focus on the child who has passed, and the guilt will continue to build and create its own obstacles to the grieving process and the eventual acceptance of the loss.

An adult who loses a child may have more opportunities for interaction with others who have also lost children. This adult may also have opportunities to talk to others of the same age who have known others who have gone through similar situations. Other adults who have lost a child and adults who have supported a friend through such a loss can both be reliable friends to talk to at various times throughout the day.

However, when a younger person loses a sibling, other relative, or friend, they often feel isolated because they have no experience or background to draw on in dealing with a similar death. They may have lost a grandparent or a friend's parent or even their own parent, but very often they have no experience of losing a young person. So, this is relatively new to them, and their emotions are still trying to find their way in order to work out what has happened. Sometimes children who witness the passing of another child have difficulty accepting the crossing. At other times they're more attuned with what is happening and understand the events more quickly following a child's passing than that of an adult. By this, we mean that children are usually more accepting of the outcome than adults. They don't add all the extra anxiety and possibilities that adults do when losing someone before their expected time. We see this especially with adult children. Many times, they accept the fact of the passing more quickly than the parents do. This is because they are at a stage of their lives when things are constantly in flux. Changes may be occurring due to starting families, job changes, and perhaps moving to different locations, whereas parents may have stabilized their living and working situations and are not used to major changes. At the same time, when a child passes over, the parents may have more time to analyze the situation and its possible meanings than an adult child whose attention, responsibilities, and activities may be dictated by their current lifestyle.

Interactions with Others

People are often concerned about the relationship between parents and their child. These concerns may be affected by how the child crossed, and some people may judge the parents as the cause of the child's crossing. This is unfortunate, as the family unit has been traumatized and will continue to be influenced by the passing. Oftentimes people outside the family unit will add to the stress unnecessarily. Well-meaning loved ones and associates can often influence the energies of the parents. These influences can be positive, well-meaning, and healing. At other times, they can be distractions as well as downright impolite.

We wish to focus on the positive. When a parent reaches out to others after the loss of a child, they may be seeking many different kinds of support. Some want comfort and understanding, while others want assistance in their daily living. Some wish simply to have someone to talk to, while others hope that others will intervene and take up the slack of their lives when they are unable to perform certain tasks.

So, there are different roles that can and must be filled by these loving souls who wish to interact with the family unit. Their intentions are sometimes of great concern, as they may lack knowledge of how to go about these tasks.

Sometimes they will seek out parents and ask what they can do to be of service, as they are not sure what priorities the parents need help with. Some will extend their time, finances, and love, depending on the parents' current needs and what they are capable of accepting.

Other times, they will take it upon themselves to act in accordance with their traditions and past experiences and will help in that manner. An example is a neighbor preparing a meal for the family without consulting them. Realizing that the family is grieving and has their hands full, the neighbor wishes to take the burden of feeding the family off the shoulders of the caregivers.

Not all adults are capable of receiving all the help that is available to them. For various reasons, they may wish to remain isolated from people outside the family unit. When this happens, the isolation can cause much disruption in the healing process as well as instances of self-pity. This is not unusual and is very common when a child passes before their perceived time. Humans do not understand the complex nature of younger individuals passing before the adult's matured age. Those suffering the loss of a child seek out what comforts them the best, be it isolation, staying busy, or even overindulging in a particular activity that may not be healthy or even satisfying.

Many times, wonderful people wish to interact with the family to remind them of the wonderful joy and love they experienced before the child passed. These interactions and conversations can be very healing on many levels, as they remind the family of the true spirit of the child who has crossed over. Oftentimes these stories consist of much joy, laughter, and love. This is where the real healing and the real interaction between the groups have the greatest opportunity to see who we really are.

It is in these times of sharing stories that the true essence of love comes forth. The lack of judgment is also an important issue in these conversations. At this time, many will not be concerned about the possible negative attributes of previous situations but rather will dwell more on the uplifting, more positive, and higher aspects of the child's life. This is an action that is particular to living the human experience. As people grow and understand the higher meanings of life many of these concepts will come naturally. For those people understand the true meaning of life and that is to share the joy, happiness, and love that we all create throughout our lives.

As we learn and grow through experiences in life situations, we have the opportunity to learn these qualities that people have chosen to enhance by coming to the Earth plane. How we deal with these situations is a test in our experience of living on this plane.

Some people will pass with flying colors, while others are just beginning to learn. Still others don't want to participate in this higher learning activity at all.

People have a tendency to judge others from different perspectives. Their actions can vary from keeping their distance to becoming overinvolved in a situation. These are all learning opportunities for everyone involved, including the family unit. It's important to realize that people are coming from different levels of understanding. Some may come across as uncaring, but that is simply the level they are currently at. Hopefully with time they will learn to be more careful of their actions and use this awareness to increase their compassion and generosity to those who suffer.

As a parent or other loved one who has lost a child, try to keep this in mind when you may be offended by the actions of others. Hopefully, this information gives you an insight into where they're coming from. They come from an area of lack, unknowing, and even ignorance. To protect yourself from the consequences of these types of situations, it's okay to isolate yourself from these particular individuals. Your reasoning is an understanding that, at this particular time, you can be swayed by your emotions and physiological changes within your body. Once things have calmed down and have become more reliable, you are free to reflect upon the interactions you had with others concerning the passing. But remember that people come from different perspectives, and we don't want you to be hurt by not taking this into account. By including this explanation, we hope that your healing can be uninterrupted by the interactions of some of these individuals.

At other times, you have a responsibility to yourself to accept the generosity and love from those around you. Even if you do not "feel like it," it is a wise choice to let some of these people into your inner space. It gives those who wish to help a growing opportunity to increase their soul's knowledge of love and compassion by helping others. It also helps your soul understand the higher meanings of life, such as being able to accept help and love from sources outside of the family unit. It can create a healing balm to the turbulent emotional changes that are going on throughout your physical body.

Relying on others at a time of passing will not make you less of a person, parent, or caretaker. It just shows that you have the ability to accept and trust loving-kindness from others.

The mingling of energies from those who wish to help and the energy you are currently established in creates a type of love that is very special. This is a very fine, pure love. It's the kind of love you only find when people lower their barriers and protection in an effort to help relieve the suffering of those involved.

At times this may be easier than at other times. It truly is a one-on-one situation that depends on the individuals' makeup and cultural experiences. Do not be disturbed if events surrounding the passing bring up emotional trauma from other experiences. This can cause a complex series of interactions between others that aren't necessary at that time. In other words, it's best if you stick to one particular situation at a time. This will help the body and emotional being not become overcome by multiple events that have transpired in the past. An example is someone bringing up a situation from the past that may or may not have anything to do with the current situation. In this case, it's not necessary and only adds additional burden to the present.

Try not to get caught up in that comparison as it will only intensify the grief and create a cycle of judgment and unanswerable questions.

Discussing with Other Children

It is advisable for an adult to sit down with living children and discuss the passing of a child. This can be done in an open forum with interaction between multiple children. When we say children, we mean younger people; we do not want to put an age limit on the term *children*. At times a one-on-one discussion may be more beneficial to both people involved. Younger people, even though they may have less experience with the passing of loved ones, have special qualities in dealing with these transitions. They have an inner strength that is not always evident but can come to their aid at these times. They may also have verbal and physical ways to act on their emotions, such as visiting with friends and organizing events around the passing of the loved one. Many times you see this with younger children gathering flowers at the place of the deceased, holding a fundraiser, or creating a memorial with their friends to show support as well as receive support that is being offered.

However, the interaction between an adult and a child is separate and different from interactions between two or more adults or between two or more children. So, as an adult, time should be spent with children to discuss the events around the passing as well as to answer any questions they may have surrounding the event. This should be done in as open a way as possible. Even if the conversation is one-on-one, it should proceed as if it's between adults. This helps remove the mystifying aspect of death.

All the children involved will still have many questions—spiritual, emotional, and mental—about the whole situation, but you don't want to create more of a disturbance by not being open and straightforward with those who have experienced the same loss. By being open, you actually begin to heal each other.

By interacting with others who share this loss, you can begin to heal yourself. It is not necessary to talk to each other from your own individual perspective. In other words, a parent does not necessarily have to talk about the deceased from a parent's point of view, and a sibling does not necessarily have to talk about the departed from the sibling's point of view. Shared memories can be used to access the healing between the two individuals. Concerns that one or both of you may have can also be worked out or just talked out between the two of you.

It is important to understand that the perspective you hold about losing a child should not be pushed onto other children or young adults. This will just add to their confusion and is not necessary. A sibling or a young person who has lost a friend does not need the extra uncertainty of how to deal with a passing and also how to deal with an adult who is dealing with the same passing. The reason is that the child can then begin to take on emotions that affect the relationship between the adult and the child who has passed. The healing process can become convoluted and more emotions and experiences intermingled because of the hierarchy of the relationship between the two. It is best to stay out of or away from this type of interaction because it brings on unnecessary burden and grief to the situation.

Talk to each other as friends and ask how you can help each other. Let the other know you're available to talk at any time or a specific time. Do not isolate each other. This does not mean you should not give space to others. Each person will grieve in their own time and at their own level. Some may need solitude in order to digest what has happened and how to proceed. This is healthy, to a certain extent. However, we do not want someone to be isolated to the point where they are dealing with all this emotion and awareness by themselves for an extended period of time. Just checking in on them once in a while can be a valuable healing experience. It delivers the message that you care for the other person and are also giving them time and space to deal with the situation on their own. But you are also available to them.

If multiple children are involved, such as a number of siblings, they will also interact with each other in order to question what has happened. This is normal and expected. Much healing can occur through interactions between siblings or friends at this level. Often time's siblings may isolate themselves and begin to show signs of hiding their feelings or deepening their pain. This is something that other siblings as well as parents should keep an eye on so it does not create more problems in the physical world.

There is also a dynamic of females being able to help other females at a different level of progression than males might be able to do. Of course, this depends on different cultures, religions, and social situations. But at times when discussing these types of situations with other women, there is a feeling of connection and bonding that can also help in the healing process.

When more than one child works together in interacting with an adult, the power and connection are multiplied. By this, we mean that if two children are working in tandem, they have the opportunity to create more open lines of communication and possibilities for healing with the adult. The children may feel more confident talking together after discussing the events individually.

The main theme with this particular question is interaction with others as it affects your own grieving process. In order to do this, it's best to do it as openly as possible while also taking into consideration other people's levels of grieving. As we stated earlier, some may seek isolation more than others. But no matter what, there should be some interaction among all involved, and this should continue for some time after the passing. It can be scheduled, spur of the moment, or just touching base, as you would say, to let the others know you're still thinking of them and you still care.

This works from child to adult as well as from adult to child. So, don't be afraid to interact with others who may not be on the same level in terms of age or socially or emotionally. Let them know you care about how they are dealing with their grief, and keep the lines of communication open. This will allow for the greatest healing opportunity you will have for many years to come.

Be aware of others. Know when to interact as well as when to step back. But do not isolate anyone, as they will feel as though they have been left alone. A little contact goes a long way. And this should be ongoing—not just in the days and months after the passing. It should continue for years and even a lifetime.

We hope this puts this question into perspective and takes away some of the feelings of guilt or confusion about how to interact with others during a time of loss. Openly, considerately, and compassionately.

Children's Insights

Benjamin

Hi, my name is Benjamin. I was sixteen years old when I passed. I'm glad to be here to share my story with you so that other kids' parents will understand what we went through and how we are making out now. I'm not going to go into the details of how I passed because it's not really necessary. It's basically that something happened to my system that affected my organs, and that's how I passed.

After I came over to this side, I realized that this side is my real home. This is the place where I came from. See that place over there? That's my house where I live now. (He shows me a house up on a slope.) People think that heaven is this crazy, wild place with flying angels and lollipops. But it's really not that way—it's more like your side on a nice day with perfect weather and no responsibilities to anyone but yourself. But there are responsibilities because there are things you want to accomplish in life, like learning and interacting with your side and understanding how the process of going to the Earth plane can help in one's development.

So, there's plenty of time for fun. I can play games with my friends, and I can watch other people perfecting their skills, like doing music, learning building skills, and studying medicine. These are the kinds of things people work on perfecting over here so that when it's time, if they decide to come to your existence, they will already have background and experience in these things.

So, when you're born on the Earth plane, you have these talents already built into you, and sometimes they come out somewhere along your life path. Sometimes they won't, depending on whatever decisions you have made before you decided to come back. But I won't get into that right now; I just want to let you know that we are busy on this side working on things that we enjoy and that can also bring us great fun and peace as well as ways to help people on your side.

Tracy is my sister, and I want to say hi to her. She's older now, and she's doing very well. I look over her and help her with some of her decisions—mostly inner confidence. These are the types of things we can do on this side—things like inspiring someone, helping with their confidence, and showing them that they are loved.

Love all you guys, and thank you for letting me contribute.

Robert

Hi Joe. My name is Robert, but my friends call me Bobby. I was older than a lot of the kids who have come through so far when I passed. I was nineteen when I crossed, but I had many experiences before that which added to my age. I was older than my nineteen years. Some people have many more experiences than others at the same age, and this was true in my case. I experience things that most people don't until they're in their thirties. So that's what I meant by being older than some of the children who have come through.

I had a learning disability that set me back during the years that I was on the Earth plane. I had difficulty understanding words, and my writing was off, too. My hearing was fine, and I could talk okay, but I had problems communicating. It was very frustrating to get across what I was trying to say. Sometimes people would be upset that they couldn't understand me, and this caused a lot of stress and grief for me and my parents.

When I came to this side, I realized that my disability is something I wanted to share with others when I was alive on the Earth plane. I decided before I was born that I would take on this disability in order for others to learn how to deal with people who are not like themselves. So when people became frustrated with my lack of ability to communicate, they learned how to accept me and work with me to help me achieve what I was trying to get across. They showed a lot of compassion after learning that the frustration they experienced was not healthy and did not create the love that they wanted to share with me.

So I wanted to share this with you to let you know that many times people will take on certain disabilities in order to help teach others about self-love, compassion, and empathy. I didn't realize this when I was on the Earth plane, but I did see the shift and growth from those around me who accepted my disability and worked with me. A special bond was created between us that continues to this day. I still feel that love on this side, and I send my love and knowledge back to them in order to help them in their new experiences. There is more two-way communication than people realize from our side to your side, and yes, even from your side to our side. By keeping your heart open, the connection is made easier than by not believing it's possible. I especially wanted to share today that we are all still connected.

Christopher

Hi Joe, my name is Christopher. I'm glad to be able to talk with you today. I was asked if I wanted to contribute something to this cause, to your book. I thought about it for a while and decided that I thought it was necessary to talk about how we feel when we cross over after we have been adopted. Many times we are not aware of our biological parents when on the Earth plane, but once we arrive back on this side, we know who they were. It's much easier to understand from this perspective how the roles of those who bring us up can differ from one's biological parents. Three of the four people involved in my life were aware of their roles before they came. My new mother—the adoptive mother—was not. She took on the role of my mother because of the influence my father had on her. She was presented with the situation of an adoption being made available, and she was open to discussing it with my adoptive father.

His main goal on the Earth plane was to help facilitate my experiences when I showed up and to give my adoptive mother opportunities to learn and grow through the act of adoption. She would learn how to take care of a child who was not biologically her own and learn to love it and cherish it as if it were. Her love and compassion are as strong as any biological mother's could have been. She treated me like any parent would treat their own child. She sacrificed for me, deciding to give up opportunities that would have enhanced her status among her peers in order to give me a better chance in life. In doing this, her growth was greatly accelerated because the acts of love she created around me were her choices and her choices alone.

So, I wanted to explain that certain situations that happen early in life are planned but not necessarily carved in stone. My life is an example of this; some situations were preplanned and, as I mentioned, my adoptive mother used her free will to take on the experience of adopting a child.

My passing created other opportunities for learning for those who came in contact with my adoptive mother. She learned that some people had put restraints on love and that some people deserve it in different quantities than others. She was not allowed to fully engage in her grief in public because some people did not understand the bond we shared due to the fact that I was adopted.

This created learning opportunities for both her and those she came in contact with. Some people helped my mother with her grief and accepted her as a true mother, while others challenged her grief because I was not her biological child.

I wanted to bring this up so people understand that losing a child can be extremely devastating to nonbiological parents. Many times adults will have to hide their grief out of reasonable fear that they will be judged. Love is love—do not put restraints on it. If you care for someone who has lost a child, support them with all the compassion and love in your heart no matter the circumstances of the relationship between the adult and child.

Sign Stories

Everyone Gets a Shirt

I was going through my signs from Doug, and even though it might be hard to follow, it was so incredible to me that I just had to share. My husband and I went to a conference at the A.R.E. in Virginia Beach with our two adult girls. Several mediums were there, and we had a great trip. The girls wanted to go out to dinner for sushi one night. This was hard for Scott and me because this was always what we would go out to dinner for as a family when Doug was alive. This would be the first time going without him. It was difficult, but we were glad we went. When I got home, I had a package delivered. In it were five white shirts with a picture of sushi and the words "I love goods." I did not order this! When I looked at my credit card account, I saw that I was charged and then immediately refunded without my ever having contacted them! I contacted the company, but they never responded to my email. I went to their website. It was a company where you could design your own shirts. As I was looking through some of their samples, the last one caught my eye: "I'm not just a Mom, I'm a Mom to a child with Wings." I don't know how he did it, but I just KNEW Doug was behind this incredible sign.

I also forgot to mention that there is significance to it being five shirts. With Doug, there are five members in our family! I sometimes wonder if he was in cahoots with some other spirit kid and another parent out there received mystery shirts! Yes, it was definitely one of my favorite signs.

Scott and Robin Brown

Author
Spirit loves to use specific times or events when sending a group sign. It's their way of showing that they are still involved in their loved ones' lives. Kids can be very creative and get a real kick out of some of the ways to send a sign. I agree with Robin on this one—Doug probably was in cahoots with others to pull this off. And somewhere out there, someone else is asking themselves, "Who ordered these shirts?" Hopefully they recognized their sign.

Sibling Signs

I am the mother of two adult children on the other side. They both died at age twenty-nine, two and a half years apart. On my fiftieth birthday, a year and a half after my daughter died, I opened my sock drawer and found a sticky note lying on top that was written by my daughter that said, "Laci loves Mommy." There was a time when she cleaned the house for me and left these sticky notes everywhere. I had saved one in my sock drawer, but it would have been underneath everything else.

About a week after my son died, I was still on bereavement leave and decided to clean out my closet to give myself something to do. At the back of the closet, I found a box of school papers and things that I had saved from the kids. Near the top of that pile was a note from my son that said, "Thanks for loving me, Mom. Love, John."

I am not terribly in tune with my surroundings, so I guess the kids have to hit me over the head with something in their own handwriting to get me to pay attention!

In memory of Laci and John

Author

This is a great example of using a sign that has worked in the past. The fact that John followed Laci's lead and sent a very similar sign shows how they are together and how they decided that "Mom will really get it if it's the same." It made the connection stronger and more obvious, and therefore successful. It also shows that children who have passed know what's going on in our lives, as Laci's sign was on her mom's fiftieth birthday!

Blinking Lights

I wanted to share one of my favorite signs from Aymen. It happened the same weekend that I attended Suzanne Giesemann's class in NM where Aymen came through. Suzanne gave me a reading that changed my life forever. That same weekend, my two daughters, Nadia and Laila, were together in NYC. They were going to a Coldplay concert. They bought tickets off of Craigslist and got amazing floor seats.

Right after Aymen's Celebration of Life ceremony, the girls were together and the song "Yellow" by Coldplay was playing and the lights started blinking on and off. They would say, "Aymen, if that is you, blink the lights." The lights kept blinking. They knew it was Aymen.

On the way to the concert, Laila called her friend and said she hoped they played the song "Yellow," which she associated with her brother. Right before the concert, the girls called me crying because the tickets they bought on Craigslist were fake. I told them to calm down and go to the box office to see if there were any more seats. They said it was a waste of time because the concert had been sold out for months. I told them to go check and I would get them the new tickets. To their amazement, two tickets had become available, and they were floor seats and better than the first ones!

As they entered the stadium, each person was given a digital wristband that turned different colors, and all the wristbands were in color sync together. The third song that the band played was "Yellow." So, all of the wristbands in the entire MetLife Stadium (fifty thousand people) turned yellow and stayed yellow through the entire song... all the wristbands but Laila's! Laila's stayed red for the entire song. Then after the song "Yellow" was over, it functioned in sync with everyone else's.

Simply amazing! I have short clip that Nadia took showing Laila's wristband staying red while everyone's wristbands were yellow.

Yes, our children are always with us and can give us incredible signs. We love you, Aymen Soussi. Keep sending us signs!

In memory of Aymen Soussi
By his mother, Tracy Soussi

Author

The fact that the girls were able to get such prized seats at that time was a manipulation of the ticketing process. Those seats most likely were not even seen as being for sale until they had inquired as to the possibility of availability. The out-of-sync color of wristband is another example of electronic manipulation, as Aymen had done on the other occasion when the song "Yellow" played and the lights flickered. Once you recognize a sign and acknowledge it, a loved one will try to use the same or similar sign in the future. They don't have to put so much energy into gaining your attention, as it's already there from a previous event.

Sign In the Clouds

Our son Zachary Braden Collins was born on September 6, 1997. He was diagnosed with stage four neuroblastoma on April 15, 1999. He passed away on February 7, 2002, from this cancer. Fourteen years after his passing, our family went to Virginia in August for a vacation. It was a beautiful day without a cloud in the sky and with golden rays from the sun beaming down. As we were driving around sightseeing on Skyline Drive, I had a sense come over me to pull over in a particular spot to admire the view and take pictures as a family. As I was taking the pictures, I noticed what appeared to be an image of a child in a cloud. This cloud in particular resembled a previous picture taken of my son before he passed away. We took many pictures but only one appeared with an image of a child. It was at that moment that I knew Zachary was sending us a sign from heaven for my husband's and my twenty-fourth anniversary. When the vacation was over, we returned home. I couldn't wait to dig out the picture that matched the image that was in the cloud. Sure enough, they matched. The Lord works in mysterious ways. We are blessed and thankful for the gifts God gives and the joy of Zachary in our lives.

In precious memory of Zachary Braden Collins

Author
Many times we see messages in nature that resonate with us at a particular time. Here is an example where a family got to enjoy a shared sign and record it, too. Zachary knew how to present himself so he would be noticed, with an image already embedded in his mom's consciousness from years earlier. It's also another example of connecting on a special day, their anniversary. Nice job, Zachary!

A Heart

Our daughter, Jordan, passed over three years ago. She started sending us signs days after she left here. Her dad and I thank her each time. We talk about her every day because she is still right here. She's creative with her signs for us. If we ask her for something specific, she delivers. Yesterday was our thirtieth wedding anniversary. All weekend, we felt her near. Last night as we were heading off to bed, a bright white heart appeared on our dining room wall above a picture of us. Bill and I were covered with chills as we looked in amazement. How could this be? Bill said, "Don't question it—just accept that it's from Jordan." Nothing in our home has been moved in order to have a heart-shaped shadow appear. We finally realized she had moved one track light on a twelve-foot ceiling in our living room to make it bounce off a heart-shaped mirror in the den so it could reach its destination on the dining room wall next to our precious picture. This was the most spectacular anniversary gift we've ever received—the perfect gift from our girl, who has filled our hearts to the brim with her love and attention. We are so thankful. We love you, Jordan.

Bill & Michele Tillery
In memory of our daughter, Jordan Brooks

Author

It's so amazing how our loved ones show us they are still around, especially on certain occasions. One of the reasons they have had the ability to recognize, so any signs from Jordan is referenced in how Bill initially commented on the sign, "Don't question it—just accept that it's from Jordan." What great advice—something to remember and put into practice.

Ribbons

After my sister passed away, I recall tirelessly asking for signs—for some sort of symbol or sign of presence aside from glimmers in sunsets and butterfly encounters. I recall asking for encounters, to hear her voice, or anything that might bring the feeling of her company again. I stayed up late many nights during this time. One particular night, I was sitting in bed around 2:00 a.m. listening to soft music. There were ribbons hung on the wall behind me, above my headboard.

I was thinking of my sister, and then I stopped hyperfocusing on the moment. Out of the blue, two of the ribbons that were nailed to the wall behind me flew off the wall and halfway across the room. Though I was taken aback at the moment, I knew this was my sister Karla giving me the sign I'd been asking for.

In memory of Karla

Author

In this case, Karla decided to create a very apparent sign. The movement of objects takes a lot of energy, but they can be very effective, as we see here with her sister's response.

Karla has mastered the ability to move objects, as we can see in these two stories. She has had this ability from very early in her passing. I know this because I have witnessed it firsthand.

After being contact by Karla's parents to give them a reading, I set up a Skype session. As Karla come through and began to answer some very important questions the parents had surrounding her passing, I noticed something behind both of them move. It seemed like the top of an extended suitcase handle went by from the left of them across their backs to the right and off the screen. I stopped the reading and asked, "Did something just move behind you?" They said, "Did you see that?" I said, "Yes, was it the top of an extended suitcase handle?" and they replied, "No, it was the top of an extended handle of a rolling briefcase." Right in the middle of the reading, we all smiled and confirmed that it was Karla. So, after receiving this sign story from Karla's sister, I wasn't surprised to see that Karla enjoyed moving objects as one of her methods of contact.

The Rose

Yesterday on New Year's Eve while I was working, I was thinking about Kevin's funeral, which was also held on New Year's Eve. I was remembering that, when we were in the chapel, I started handing out flowers from the arrangements. As I was thinking about this, I went on my break and went to the bathroom to wash my hands. There, sitting on top of the hand dryer, was a single red rose—the same type of flower I was handing out at Kevin's service. I believe in signs and how they come when we need them most. Love you, Kevin. Thank you so much for your amazing signs.

Jen, in memory of my son, Kevin

Author

Jen has a great connection to her son, Kevin, and he does come through relatively easily. She learned early to notice and accept these signs, so that has helped with the connection.

Section IV

Guilt & Suicide

"After I came over to this side, I realized that this side is my real home. This is the place where I came from."

J.M.Higgins

Guilt

Guilt is a conflict between an individual's mind and soul. The mind will constantly replay a situation and will overrule the connection the individual has to their soul. As they continue to play out the feelings of guilt, it just reinforces the mind to continue with the same conclusion, even though it is not correct. Being aware of this can help a person begin to break out of the guilt process and move forward into healing, understanding, and peace.

As we mentioned before, the soul comes to the Earth plane with many tools and abilities to deal with situations and events that take place on the human level. But as we see with guilt, the human experience can corrupt the connection to the soul. Guilt can take on a life of its own. It can take over one's life plan and keep it from growing as it should.

Once you understand the power that guilt can have over oneself, you can begin to see how taking away its power can bring relief and healing. Just considering this idea can begin the process of releasing you from the chains of guilt.

Oftentimes people who are experiencing a great deal of guilt have separated themselves from others on the Earth plane. Not only is that an injustice to themselves but also to those who come to the Earth experience to interact with them. Their individual life plans must be altered because of the guilt-ridden person's inability to interact with them. The interactions of souls take place on multiple levels and through multiple situations. But isolation due to guilt can cause you to lose the ability to interact with those who may need you. Your healing and understanding are needed for the interactions with others that will play out in your future.

Let yourself learn at a pace that is best for you. Some may learn quicker, while others may take longer to understand the process of releasing their guilt back to the universe. It is an individual journey, but you are not alone on that journey. The love and support surrounding you are immense from our side and are often quite strong from your side as well. Be aware of this and keep in mind that you have the ability to heal yourself by just opening your heart and allowing the love and compassion of others to start the process. There is an expression "Let go and let God." This is a great example of releasing your hold on guilt and allowing the love that flows from our side and from your fellow humans to interact with your heart and to start the healing process that you so richly deserve.

Could I Have Done Something Differently?

~~~~~

Joe, this is a question we are often asked by those who feel they could have made a difference in stopping someone from crossing over.

There are many aspects to a crossing, and they depend on each individual. Some may have preplanned their crossing, some may have taken advantage of an early exit, and others will pass due to the judgment of free will. What all of these have in common is that the individual who crosses over is in charge, to a certain degree.

Although others can play an important part in the transition, it's not always required that they partake in the decision to cross over. By this, we mean that a parent may be involved in the child's development and may have exposed the child to a dangerous activity that caused the death of the child. The adult may feel that they were responsible for the loss of the child when, in fact, that child may have decided to leave at that particular time and created the opportunity through the parent to have that exit appear so they could transition. There are many examples of this type of interaction, but it is important to remember that parents don't always have the answers. Some may feel that their actions or inaction caused the transition of the child, but it's not as simple as that. There are other complex mechanisms happening around transitions.

So, it is very important that we tell parents, other loved ones, and those who have interacted with children that things are not as they seem. Their actions may seem to have caused or aided in the transition of a child, but we know that the parents and guardians are not aware of all the circumstances around a particular death.

So, the fact is that there is nothing you could have done differently to change the outcome that happened. If your actions had caused the child to miss an opportunity to cross over, a new exit opportunity would have appeared, and the child would have had the ability to take that one. A parent's decision will not affect the child's path and decision to cross over. It may seem as though you are protecting the child while helping them grow and learn about the physical world. To a certain extent, you are. Your teachings can help a child avoid certain lessons that do not need to be learned. So, your protection and guidance are highly valued. But when it comes to a major decision-action such as crossing back over to the spirit plane, your influence is not as important as you may think. It is the same with some health issues, as they may have been "penciled in" before birth to be taken advantage of if warranted. We understand that we keep referring to this concept but it is important to understand so we try to state it in several different ways.

In your terms, you protect and teach a child to avoid harm's way regarding both little and big things—the daily interactions that you believe can bring pain and suffering. **However, you did not have control over the child's transition.**

So, if you think you could have done things differently, you couldn't have. You are cursing yourself and beating yourself up over something you truly had no control over. You may think you had control, but in actuality there was more at play, and you had no control. It is very important to realize this fact so you can begin the process of healing from the burden of self-punishment that many of you force on yourself on a daily basis. This suffering is unnecessary and can stunt your spiritual growth while on the Earth plane.

Your love for your child is so great that you believe you let them down and to some extent caused their passing. You believe that someone must pay for this, and ultimately you convict yourself. You become judge, jury, and executioner. You play these mind games over and over, creating a loop of punishment that seems to go on forever. Many times people's lives become stagnant because their self-worth has diminished to the point where they feel that they are worthless. You are your toughest critic. This is understandable because you did not know the circumstances of what transpired on a spiritual level. But now that you know, it is important that you start to heal yourself from this self-inflicted prison you have sent yourself to.

As we have said before and will continue to say, grief is a natural emotional reaction to the passing of a loved one. It is healthy to go through the grieving steps and come to accept what has transpired. Some will have a more difficult time than others. But this in itself brings opportunities for growth, not only for the grieving person but also for the people around them who wish to interact with them and help them. So, there are always lessons going on. Some we design, and some emerge from opportunities that are created by others' actions.

But the pain that individuals put themselves through is not necessary. It is normal to try to analyze the circumstances of a passing and consider what you could have done to change them. But once you realize that there were circumstances you were not aware of, you must realize that your part has diminished. Therefore, the guilt also needs to diminish.

The guilt and suffering that you put yourself through cause a ripple effect with those around you. It even reaches the spiritual side. The child can see the grieving that you are going through and feels anguished that their loved one is experiencing self-inflicted torment. They wish for you to know that there were other circumstances at play. This is one of the reasons we have Joe writing this book, so that the information can be distributed to those who need it. Once these concepts are understood, it's our intention to facilitate some of the healing that needs to take place in order for the grieving loved ones to continue on their current path. For if they continue to punish themselves, certain opportunities will not be able to be created for them to learn and enjoy.

Take the energy that you put into your self-doubt about your actions and turn it into a loving, healing balm to be used daily on yourself. This healing will open up other opportunities for you to grow and to help not only yourself but others as well. It will allow you to deal with the transition on a different level. It will give you opportunities to remember your loved one who has passed in a different light.

Heal yourself and love yourself. It is necessary for you to create the loving life that you deserve.

Suicide

"Joe, we know this is a difficult subject for many people, especially those who have been touched by the death of a loved one in this manner. Suicide is a complex event focusing on one individual but having repercussions beyond that individual's perspective. You see, when a person decides to take their own life, it jeopardizes events not only in their life to come but also people who interact and are associated with the victim.

"Many times the person who takes his own life does not fully understand what is happening to them and the purpose of their life. They are confused as to the nature of their being and why it is necessary to live out their path." [From *Always Connected for Veterans*]

A suicide may occur when opportunities for growth become overbearing to the extent that the soul is not able to incorporate all the situations as they play out. These are times when the soul may become confused as to its purpose in this incarnation. When the soul becomes confused at a soul level, it can cause a dramatic change not only in the life plan but also in the larger soul plan.

Oftentimes people will not be able to continue on the Earth plane under these circumstances. We see this play out in the act of suicide.

The intentions when coming to the Earth plane were well and good, but in the playing out of the life lessons the soul is overwhelmed by the challenges they took on.

At certain times the human body will experience illnesses in various forms. Some of these may be preprogrammed into the life plan before birth to help create opportunities for growth by the individual and for others. Depression and other forms of mental illness could fall under this category. Illnesses caused by trauma and other situational events can be acquired during one's life and are not necessarily preplanned. However, at times both of these types of afflictions may cause too much of a disruption of the mind/soul connection and cause isolation in the human experience.

Not knowing how to deal with this overwhelming challenge, the human individual takes over the entire process of decision-making. The insights that the soul has will become blocked, and the tools that the soul has brought to the Earth plane are not able to be used. At times the tools themselves have not been integrated into the soul fully before being born. The human environment and conditions are then the only sources of reason and decision-making. Under these circumstances, the individual is not allowed to see the bigger picture because they become shut off from their soul connection. It is like losing radio contact with an individual and then that individual having to make decisions without knowing all the facts.

When an individual is in this particular state of mind, their decision-making abilities are corrupted. Their free will choices cannot tap into insights they may need to function correctly, so they become unregulated and indiscriminate. This is what leads many to take their own life.

It is this suffering and the inability to see a solution that create an environment where suicide is the only considered option. This not only affects the soul but also affects those around it. Some of the effects of those who are connected to such an event can be worked into their life plan. This particular situation has not been set up before they arrived, but it can be used to learn certain important experiences, such as self-love, compassion for others, and how to bring awareness of this problem when individuals feel lost and unconnected.

The individual soul that returns to the spirit realm after committing suicide is greeted with love and compassion. They realize upon arriving that they could not make critical decisions at the time when they took their life. Often when realizing this, they understand that they wish they had not completed the act. For now they have a different perspective, and they can see how and why it played out. But from their new perspective, they also see that, on the Earth plane, they did not have the opportunity to see the bigger picture. They will begin to learn self-love for having taken their own life and will realize that they did not have the tools to continue to live on the Earth plane. *[A young man named Kevin who passed by suicide explained this to his mother during a reading, stating "Mom, I didn't know how to handle things. I left my tool box in the truck."]*

They are surrounded with love and compassion, and will continue to learn how this experience has played out. This soul will go through special training to integrate the original tools for coping with experiences on the Earth plane. Once these tools are integrated back into the soul, the soul will have an opportunity to reenter the Earth plane at a time of its choosing. The individual once reborn will have a stronger connection to it soul and therefore to its natural abilities to deal with life's situations.

People who witness such events are often traumatized to such a degree that their soul has been affected. By affected, we mean that the event is not only a lesson to be observed but has also traumatized the soul. These individuals will need special attention by those on the Earth plane as well as loved ones on the other side. Love and compassion can and will flow freely from all those individuals on both sides to the individual who is suffering due to the interaction with the suicidal event.

This is when it is very important that the individual who has been left behind and traumatized by such an event is open to receive love and compassion. This will enable the individual to regain balance over their life plan and to be able to continue in their growth in helping others to learn as well as themselves. There will be many opportunities for growth and healing after a suicide if the individual takes the opportunity to access them.

These opportunities can take the form of learning to take care of themselves and learning that their life is just as precious as everyone else's. Compassion for themselves is very important as well as sharing love with others who have had similar experiences. By surrounding themselves with like-minded individuals, the healing can take place faster and deeper. Like-minded individuals will help in the healing because they will be at different levels of growth concerning this type of event. Some may have lost an individual many years prior, while others may have lost someone more recently. These various levels of experience allow everyone to aid each other in their healing. Those who wish to heal on their own are given equal opportunity to do so. It is not necessary to interact with like-minded individuals in order to heal. However, it is an option that many seek out and are happy that they have.

An individual wishing to heal should understand that it may take many years and experiences to come to terms with a suicide. Some of these experiences will be integrated into an individual's life's plan, so the time taken in recovery is not limited or lost. Learning experiences will become available as they continue to grow on the Earth plane.

It's important for individuals to realize that they're not alone in their grief and misunderstanding. There are avenues for them to access information and support on the Earth plane, and they will be led to these once they open their heart and accepted that they are on a healing journey. Unfortunately, the human body can counteract some of these opportunities, as certain chemical reactions may take place and change an individual's ability to appreciate the opportunities for healing that are presented to them.

This is why it's very important for individuals to take care of themselves. This means acts of self-love, realizing the continuation of growth, and not taking control of the situation that happened. Oftentimes we see this result in guilt, which will hinder healing and growth.

Parents & Suicide

❦

When people lose a loved one—in this case, a child—to suicide or through other means, they at times consider giving up their own life in order to be with the one who passed.

Many times when a loved one crosses over, suddenly there are human factors that come into play. By this, we mean there are chemical reactions, emotions, and other biological responses that take place in those left behind.

As with someone who ends their own life, many who are associated with the tragic passing begin to lose focus and perspective on their own life. Some people are so traumatized by the loss that they no longer wish to carry on. They no longer see the sense in continuing to live.

The only solution they believe exists is to cross over so they can continue to enjoy the loved one who has passed. They lose the perspective of how special life on the Earth plane is because they have voluntarily shut down certain information that they used previously to help them plan out their normal daily life.

When a child passes, it is not uncommon for the parents to wish to cross over to be with that child. In part, this is a result of not wanting to abandon the child even after the child's death. Sometimes there is guilt involved, and at other times the parents simply want that physical, loving connection to be reinstated.

However, this creates uncertainty within the individuals who were left behind. Their wishes and aspirations conflict with their own connection to the Earth plane. They question their existence, and they question why certain things have to take place in their life. They ask broad, open-ended questions as they try to find answers about the passing of their loved one. Emotionally, all they want is to be with that person—to be able to hold them and feel their physical love.

What they don't understand is that the physical type of love can only be experienced on the Earth plane. The love that is experienced on the other side is greater than can be explained. Love can cross the boundaries between physical life and death. However, the love that people experience on the Earth plane is a type of love that can only be experienced while alive. When one reaches the other side, love becomes a finer vibration that is more intense.

This doesn't diminish the fact that the individual at this particular time still needs a connection. It is from loving so deeply that this idea of giving up one's life in order to be with the love one is created.

There are many factors at play when someone considers crossing over to meet with a deceased loved one. The loved one on the other side does not want you to end your life due to their crossing. They feel the sorrow that you are suffering and wish to relieve it, but they are limited in what they can do because of various roadblocks. By roadblocks, we mean that oftentimes communication such as signs and feelings aren't able to get through. Even the dream state is compromised due to the shock and confusion of those left behind.

The interactions of those left behind can be abruptly changed if someone crosses over to meet with a deceased loved one. Many lives can be disrupted and soul plans may need to be altered. Using one's free will to cross back over to our side is not the purpose of an exit point and is not to be confused with a regular suicide. In other words, the purpose of crossing over to meet with someone recently deceased is to reconnect with the loved one, as opposed to an original suicide, which involves a lack of understanding that any relief from suffering exists. These individuals are unable to see any other sources of pain relief, so they close down to the point of ending their own life.

A person who deliberately crosses over to relieve their own suffering about being apart from someone who has passed takes on the additional burden of creating more suffering for those who are left behind.

These people often believe that by taking their own life, they will meet up with the deceased loved one, and everything will be as it was before. This couldn't be farther from the truth. Their life will have to be readjusted once they reach our side. By readjusted, we mean the person will realize that what they have done is not in their best interest nor the the best interest of the one who passed over before them. They will realize that they have affected the lives of those who are left behind and that their actions have corrupted many people's life plans.

When they cross over, what they experience is a different form of their loved one than the one they experienced on the Earth plane. This form may be a more enlightened individual who may seem to be an older soul who has more knowledge. The structural relationship will often not be the same. A mother who follows her child by committing suicide will realize that the mother-child dynamic is no longer in effect, unlike what would follow from the natural passing of the mother. The child could be a close friend or relative or possibly even a stranger, for the roles you play on the Earth plane are not always the same as your true essence. Once you revert back to your true spiritual home, you'll realize that the interrelationships of souls will be different from those on the physical plane.

What we're trying to say is that the expectations of the person contemplating ending their life in order to connect with the loved one who has passed are exaggerated. They think that everything will be the same and that the physical love will be able to be shared as it was before the passing. In actuality, the one who crosses seeking to be with the other will find themselves in a state of confusion and will have to deal with all the repercussions that their actions have created. Some of these repercussions include reorienting their soul plan, learning the importance of self-love, and being able to accept the terms of an experience on the Earth plane.

When it is naturally time to cross over, you will meet up with your child and be able to relive the moments and experiences that you thought were lost. If you wish, you can relive every experience from the time of the child's passing through adulthood and the senior years as if it had happened on the Earth plane. Do not think that opportunities and experiences such as marriages, graduations, birthdays, holidays, and even childbirth are necessarily lost. You will have the opportunity to experience all of these with the child who has passed when it is your time to pass naturally. This is very important to realize.

When one takes their own life to try to reconnect with a child, this ability to relive the moments that have been lost is corrupted, meaning that, due to the circumstances of your crossing, it's no longer available to you to live the life you thought you would have with the child. When you cross under these circumstances, your soul needs to be reevaluated by both you and others in order to bring peace and love to yourself before any other actions or interactions are allowed.

By crossing over through suicide in order to connect with someone else, you have created a new set of circumstances that must play out, and doing so interrupts your ability to reconnect with the child and share the wonderful milestones of life that you believe you have lost.

We do not wish to see people give up this opportunity to reconnect with children and to relive the times they thought they had lost, for it is a special moment when a loved one is reunited with their child in a way that is similar to the Earth plane experience. The souls of both will continue to grow at different levels, with the ability to interact being much easier when the adult passes naturally.

So, it is very important to learn self-love and compassion toward your own situation before passing over so you can enjoy all the possibilities that are available when it is your time to reunite with your child.

The physical and emotional pain that you must endure on the Earth plane is, in itself, a dual learning experience. For one who believes that death is the separation of love, it can create terrible grief. Once one realizes that their loved one is truly never gone and that the essence of their love continues on, this will bring relief to the emotional and spiritual heartache that is being suffered.

Children who have passed on realize what you're going through and wish to help you in your grief. They will bring people and situations into your life in order for you to be able to interact with others and realize that there is a bigger picture to life. That life can continue to grow, and bringing compassion and love to others, as well as yourself, can be a healing balm like no other.

Relieving suffering and helping others are extremely good ways to heal. Your compassion for yourself is very important to your healing process. Your ability to see the future without your child is difficult, we know, and putting pressure on yourself to see that future is not necessary. The future will play out as it needs to, and excitement, love, and new experiences that you are unaware of at the present time will play out. Your hold on the past will hold you back from experiences in the future. However, it is your free will to create the environment you wish to live in. Some will have the courage and strength to move forward, while others will need the assistance of many to make this possible.

Either way, the child will support you in your growth and will be by your side throughout your natural life. They will interact to the degree that is allowed in order to help you in your growth and healing.

From their perspective, they can understand exactly what you're going through and will make attempts to reach out to you to let you know they are still in your presence. Signs, sensing, and dreams are particular ways they will use to gain your attention.

Find strength in the love and connections with those around you who may be experiencing the same situation. Freely speak of the child who has passed and understand that they're now in a position to help you and others who have experience this type of loss.

Children's Insights to Parents on Suicide

Allison

Joe, we have Allison here, who would like to talk about what her mother went through after her passing.

Hi Joe. My name is Allison, and I was fourteen years old when I passed over.

My mom was really upset when I left, and she didn't know how to handle it at all. Oftentimes she would yell and scream at me, even though I wasn't there. She didn't understand the process of how we come to and leave the Earth plane at different times. She thought she would be able to handle my leaving much better than she did. She tried to hold on to her life as much as possible, but things began to spin out of control. She wanted to end her own life to be able to be with me again. She kept begging me to come back to be with her. Even when I was still around her, she would say things to me about how, after I left, she wanted to be with me.

I wanted to help my mom even before I died, but even more after I left. She just sat in her chair and cried all day long and didn't allow anyone to go near her. She just sat there and stared at the walls. She didn't want to be there anymore—she was done with her life. She said to me that there was nothing left in her life after I left.

When she began to say things like that, I became upset. I want to tell her that her life is precious and that there are many more precious moments to live. She couldn't see the bigger picture, but now that I have crossed, I can see her perspective. She thought the end of my life was the end of hers because she didn't realize that hers had meaning in itself. She didn't realize that she had lessons to learn and to help others learn that didn't involve me being in her life. You see, there are other things going on besides the relationship between a parent and child or an adult and child. That is just one of the things that a parent may experience. Some adults will even go on to experience much more fulfilling lives after the death of one of their children.

I want to tell my mother that she shouldn't be totally focused on me and my crossing. I want to let her know that I am okay and that I will be fine. It hurts me to see her suffer in this way. I knew she was having a human experience, but I want to tell her that we are all still connected and I can hear and feel everything that's going on with her. Her sadness has a direct line to my heart. It bring sadness to me to know she has no hope about her future. If she could only see some of the experiences she would have in the future, she would realize that there is much more to life than losing a child.

It's important for all parents who have lost children to realize it's not their time to pass, even though they may want to. It makes things very difficult on our side when this happens. A parent who passes over to see us finds out quickly that they have made a mistake. They think it will go back to the way it was before their child's passing when their child was whole and healthy. But it's not like that at all. Things change, their perspective changes, and the reality of who we are becomes known.

So, the one thing I can say to parents who are thinking about crossing over to be with their children is: don't do it. It will cause more distress to you and also to others left behind. Your expectations will not be fulfilled, and you'll actually be giving up opportunities for us to share together at a later time.

We are all still here for you and will try to make you smile and laugh like you used to before we got sick and passed. I'll try to make you giggle, Mom—I know there are certain ways to get you to do that because we used to giggle together when I was there. But first I need you to see the possibilities of a longer life and be able to enjoy it even though I'm not there. I will be by your side and help you throughout your life, as I have the ability to be with you and to continue on learning and interacting with others. The same is true of other children who have passed over.

(Anonymous)

Joe, this is from a young man who wishes to be anonymous. He wants to come through in this way because he wants to address everyone who is reading this information rather than a particular person.

Hey Joe, thank you for letting me come through and for this opportunity to talk about what we see and feel after we have passed.

Oftentimes our parents and other loved ones will go into a crazy level of grief after we pass. They go through the whole gamut of emotions, such as anger, despair, sadness, and even relief. You'd be amazed at how many parents are relieved once we have crossed. At times, they have witnessed our suffering on the Earth plane to such a degree that they wished we would cross over before we actually did.

These feelings come from love and compassion but also from the belief that we will be free of suffering once we have crossed. Oftentimes in these cases, once we have passed they realize the reality of what they had wished for. Many times they will be overcome by a sense of guilt and will begin to judge themselves about how they felt about the whole process.

This is where the human emotions get involved and have a way of messing up their minds. What they realize before the passing and what they're experiencing now do not match, so they try to make the two fit together, and this causes more stress and grief. So I want all of you to know that we understand what has happened and what you're going through, but we want to let you know that it is not necessary—that we don't wish to see you judging yourself in this way.

Your judgment comes from a place of doubt and fear of the unknown, and that's one of the reasons we all want to come through and let you know about our experiences from this side. We want you to understand the process better than you do. We believe that if you understand from our perspective, it will bring some relief to the grief you experience. If you know that we are well and happy and can still feel your love, the grief that you're experiencing will have love surrounding it and can give you an understanding of the complete process.

So, don't think about throwing in the towel, as your job is not done. We are still relying on you for certain lessons. You may think that your time on the Earth plane is not valuable anymore, but in essence it can be more valuable after a passing than before. You don't realize it, but it's true.

We will get to see each other and experience events together once again after you have passed and have fulfilled your life's obligations. Your life's obligations do not end when we pass over. So try to understand that the feelings you are experiencing are normal and that our awareness of this is constant.

We all try to help you through your grief process, but at times it's difficult because you have shut down your ability to communicate with us. Communication is done through intuition, love, and other methods.

You have an expression: *There is more to come*. This is true, and we will help you with it. Thank you for letting me try to explain the process that some parents go through.

Joe, I'd also like to add that it's impossible for parents to see us if they crossed over unnaturally right after us in order to try to be with us. There is too much corruption in the passing process, and the reason for the passing has to be corrected or reframed in order for the connection to be whole. When it is your time to pass, we will be there to greet you if you wish, but it has to be at the right time. And you don't decide the right time from the human perspective. So just a heads-up, go through the grief process and learn to love yourself and add compassion around the whole passing event. Take baby steps, and before you know it, you'll be back jogging through life, and all of us will be by your side.

Becky

This is Becky. All I want to say is, "Mom, don't do it—don't do it." It's not what you expect; there is much more going on than you realize. It's not as easy as you think. Yes, the transition can be natural, but the reasons for the transition are where it gets really murky and complex. Ending your life and coming over here to be with me is just not going to work out. It's like you coming to visit me at school, but there are other things going on that weekend. So you run into traffic and you're late, and my schedule is off and I can't get to see you, and it turns out to be a shit show — not because of your intentions but rather because of the way things work. So just plan that we will get together after it's your time to pass naturally, and we can reminisce, laugh, and create new memories together at that point. Anything before that would just be a messed-up time. I will definitely see you — we'll plan a date way in the future. Actually, it's not that far in the future because life on your plane is actually very short, though most of you don't understand that. So, do the things you have to do in your life, like you would go shopping before you would come to visit me at school, and I'll see you when you get here after a long and interesting life. Love you, and I'll be keeping an eye on you... so behave! (Says with a laugh)

Author
It's as if we've made last-minute plans and tried to force them to happen, and then they turn out crappy. We think to ourselves, "I should have just stayed home." So Becky is telling her mom to "just stay home" and they'll meet up later.

Sign Stories

The Globe

This particular sign was typical of Emma. While in the hospital, she had done a jigsaw puzzle of the world that was in the shape of a globe. It's really a nice piece because it's round. It took her hours to complete, as she was very particular and focused while putting it together. It's been very precious to me. One day, I was sitting down here next to my computer, and it fell from the top of the bookcase and rolled across the floor and landed next to my foot. I hesitated when I picked it up because I thought it was strange how it had fallen. The only part of the jigsaw that was damaged was a missing piece, India. And that was the one place that we had visited together before she was diagnosed with leukemia.

Karyn, in memory of Emma

Author
A perfectly shared memory sign—the movement of an object to gain the mother's attention, then the message conveyed by only one missing piece of a shared vacation location.

Wash Your Guilt Away

I lost my son in 2006 at the age of five from a rare form of cancer. In 2007, I gave birth to a little girl and felt so guilty for having another child and because I believed he would be upset that I had replaced him.

A week after having her, I felt really low and in despair because I had not felt that he was around. So I went to his grave, and I remember the day very clearly. It was raining hard, and I stood there crying and pleading with him to show me that he was okay and that he was not angry with me for having his sister.

The next morning was Saturday. As I was feeding my little girl, the tears would not stop falling, but I had to distract myself, so I set about doing the household chores. I loaded the dryer up, switched it on, and two minutes later the circuit breaker kicked. I switched it back on, and it did the same thing again. I thought I'd wait until my husband got up and let him sort it out. Half an hour later, my son came down and said the lights weren't working. Again the electricity kicked off, so I turned it back on. By this time, I had two loads of washing to do. My husband got up, and I told him about the dryer. He started looking at it while I went into the living room to take care of the baby. Then I heard him say, "That's weird." I came into the kitchen and asked what was weird. He said he had emptied the washer and put the next load in, and when he went to turn it back on, nothing was working, and our washer is digital. He had pulled it out, as it's in a tiny space, and the plug had been switched off at the back, which was an impossibility, as there was no room to switch it off without pulling it out. I kept thinking that our electricity was cursed.

The following day I decided to go to our spiritualist church, as I was questioning what had gone on the day before. As soon as the service began, a medium asked if she could speak to me and proceeded to tell me that a little boy (a "cheeky monkey" is how she described him) wanted to send me his love and other personal things that no one knew about and also wanted me to know that he loved me very much and that he was happy. I remember crying at the thought that he was happy. Anyway, after fifteen minutes, because he wanted to chat, she had to ask him to leave, as other people were waiting for messages from their loved ones. She proceeded to move on to another lady and asked the lady if she could speak to her. Just as the lady said yes, the medium stopped and said, "I'm sorry—he's back" (my son). She turned to me and said, "He's laughing and wants me to give you a message, but I don't understand it." She said, "He said to say 'washing machine.'" I had not spoken to anyone about the day before, as I was still trying to find another reason for it happening.

At this point, I felt elated. I knew he had heard me when I pleaded with him for a sign to tell me that he was okay and that he was not upset about his baby sister. This enabled me to move forward with some aspects of my life, knowing he was truly happy.

Sharon Starowojtow, in memory of my son

Author

Guilt can come from various actions we take as we begin to judge ourselves. Not knowing that there are bigger plans at play, many people who lose a child fall into times of guilt. Remember, you don't have all the information or insights concerning a passing. Sharon got to witness the response from her son she was looking for only after it was verified through a medium. If you ask for a sign, be open to accepting one. Look for things out of the ordinary, like this case of a washing machine switching off by itself.

My Drink & a Laugh

It was New Year's Eve, and I was at work. I became a little emotional thinking of Kevin. I wanted to cry but I didn't. I walked over to my work section and saw a pistachio martini sitting near a machine in a martini glass with no one around. It's my favorite drink, and by the way, the servers were serving drinks in plastic cups. Thank you, Kevin, for the quick uplift. Love you, miss you.

Another time, I was scrolling on Facebook in my car in a store parking lot. I read a post in one of my helping parents heal groups. A mom posted about how she asked her son for a sign and he sent her a heart. So I said, laughing, "Okay, Kevin. I'm asking you for a sign today. Two minutes later, I got out of my car to walk into the store and saw a license plate that said KGAMES, then the license plate on the car next to it said HA. Thank you so much, son. I love knowing you are always with me and listening to me. Love you, Kevin.

Jen, in memory of my son, Kevin

Author

Jen picked up a big clue, not just the type of drink, which is a great sign in itself, but also the fact that it was in a martini glass and they were only serving drinks in plastic cups that night. Well done, Kevin!

If you ask for a sign, be prepared—it just might happen right away, as it did this time. I love the sense of humor Kevin displayed as his mom kiddingly asked for a sign. He came back with two license plates to drive home his uplifting message.

Baseball & Numbers

My son Doug passed on April 18, 2015, which was my birthday. I was at work, and he had texted me "Happy Birthday, Mom. I love you." Then he died in our bathroom from a heroin overdose after being clean and happy for sixteen months. I'm learning about his soul contract, but it is so hard without him. His stepdad raised him since he was two and adopted him at age seven when we married. He loved his dad, and his dad is heartbroken, too. I did get him to see a medium with me, so that helped him. He has two stepsisters and was very, very close to them and to his sixteen-year-old niece and his three-year-old nephew (who has spinal muscular atrophy). Landon talks to him all the time. I know Doug is with him.

As for signs, I've been getting signs since Doug passed. I didn't realize it at first, but when I understood that he could give me signs, I realized that everything he was sending that upset me at first was really a sign to let me know he was okay.

He was an exceptional athlete, and the numbers he wore most were 7, 17, 22, and 99. He could throw a baseball 88 miles per hour. I get these numbers all the time, plus his birthday: 429.

When I first went to the store after he passed, I was getting cold meat and cheese for people coming over. My sister was with me. As I picked a number to be in line, the number 7 came out. I freaked out and threw it at my sister. Now I wish I had kept it. As I remember, my sister said, "Awww" with a sad look. She was very surprised, and at the time we weren't thinking about signs. But, we now sure think that was a sign. Seven was his main number through the years. He was 7 most of the time while playing baseball and hockey. It was his favorite number, along with 17. I see 717 all over at least once a day.

And because of my son's baseball life, (he played semi-pro as well), I find baseballs while I'm walking. The first time I found one, I knew it was him. I picked it up, and I felt as if he had put it in my hand. Now when I meditate, I feel him holding my hand. When I found the first baseball, I was in a field, but not during baseball season. I'd walked that same path every day with my dog, and there it was, right in the middle of the path. Then I started to find baseballs more often—sometimes just in a parking lot or near some woods.

I can be watching a sports team on TV, and all of a sudden, the numbers 7, 17, 22, and 99 are all standing there together. Crazy. Or I'll be driving and see buses with all of those numbers. I also get 11:11, 111, and 222 a lot.

In memory of Doug Paul from Mom

Author

Numbers are associated with individuals throughout their life. We have significant dates, addresses, and even uniform numbers that can be associated with an individual. When one or more particular numbers are associated with a hobby or sport, it adds to the power of the sign. We see this in Doug's sports uniforms.

Phone Call

I was grieving really bad one day and yelled at God, asking for a sign from my son. When I got up, I noticed sunlight shining onto my son's bodybuilding awards (two swords and a medallion). After I took a photo, I noticed the image of a cross aimed directly at my Bible. I live on a tree-lined street where it's impossible for the sunlight to shine through oak trees and perfectly onto my fireplace. I know it was a sign from my son because he knew that I am very spiritual.

The other sign came twenty-four hours after he transitioned. It was a call from a +0 number. He actually called me. It was later confirmed by an evidential medium. She said I couldn't hear him because he hadn't learned to make his voice audible yet.

In memory of my son, William Addison III

Author
In this sign, we see the use of modern electronic manipulation. It has become more common for people to receive phone calls from their loved ones even if the phone is off, has no battery, or is even broken.

Sense of Humor

A few years before our son, Dalton, passed away, he gave my husband a gag gift for Christmas. It was a handheld, battery-operated massager. I knew the batteries in the massager had been dead for at least six months before our son passed.

On the day before Dalton's second birthday in Heaven, I was cleaning the house and my husband was outside. I was vacuuming in the back of the house, and when I turned the vacuum cleaner off, I heard a vibrating noise coming from the living room (in the front of the house). When I went to the living room to see what the noise was, I saw that the handheld massager that Dalton had given my husband a few years earlier as a joke had turned itself on and was moving in a circle on the coffee table. My coffee mug was on the corner of the coffee table, and the massager was moving in a circle in the middle of the coffee table. I went and grabbed my phone and came back to the living room to take a picture. Then I ran outside and grabbed my husband. When we came back in the house, that's when I noticed that my coffee mug had moved to the middle of the table. The massager was moving in circles around my coffee mug. This went on for about twenty minutes until the massager fell off the table. I picked it up and tried to turn it on, but it would not come on.

I know without a doubt that Dalton turned this massager on. It was his way of letting us know he is still with us, just in a different way.

In memory of my son, Dalton Motlow

Author

This is another great example of a sign appearing on an anniversary. It was sent while both parents were home so as to resonate longer, as the two would share this new memory of their son for years to come.

GPS

I thought I would share a couple of signs that my wife and I have received from our son Bryant, whom we lost to an overdose in 2015.

About a year and a half after his passing, my wife and I were on our way to a friend's house in Northern Indiana (we live in the southeastern part). As we traveled north on Interstate 65, we were rerouted by our GPS to take a side road and continue to head north. To be honest, we never knew why it rerouted us since there wasn't a wreck or slow traffic; it just wanted us to take a different route, so we did. We ended up on Graham Avenue, which isn't all that uncommon, but what was uncommon was that as we traveled north, there was another street that intersected this road that was named Bryant. My wife was watching the GPS on her phone. It seemed as though she saw Bryant Street and I saw the green road sign with his name on it at the same time. We just looked at each other and didn't even have to say anything.

Another sign, which I received on March 26, 2017, was and is the best evidence I could ever imagine receiving from Bryant. On March 24, I was sitting in front of my computer working—I do tech support. I had been reading about talking to loved ones and asking them for signs, so I thought I would ask my son for some kind of sign to let us know he's okay and he made it over. I asked him out loud, as if he was right beside me, "Bryant, can you give me some kind of sign so I know you're okay and you're still with us?" That was on a Friday afternoon. On the following Sunday, the 26th, I was working on my taxes and had gotten bored, and I started looking through the pictures on my phone that I'd used for a fiftieth wedding anniversary video for my parents a few years back. One of those photos was taken by my mother of me at about ten years old sitting in my go-kart. That picture stayed in my mother's photo album (the big one that all mothers used to have) for thirty-plus years until I got it out a few years back to use in the video.

A little background information before I go any further: My

oldest daughter and my son raced go-karts competitively for eleven years before my father-in-law passed away at sixty from esophageal cancer. My father-in-law was instrumental in keeping my kids racing and providing anything they needed to win races. He was very, very competitive. My father-in-law was the one who chose the numbers that my kids would use on their karts for the next eleven years. I've verified it through my brother-in-law and another relative that my father-in-law chose those numbers simply because nobody else was using them at that time. The numbers were 14 for my daughter and 15 for my son.

So, fast forward, my father-in-law passed away never even knowing I had a go-kart when I was a kid, let alone ever seeing the photo I had of me in a go-kart because he passed away before I got the photo out of my mom's album to use in the video. So now fast forward to March 26, 2017. I'm going through the photos that I used in my parents' video, and I see the one of me in my go-kart when I was ten, and for some reason I think my son was guiding me because I zoomed in on the shirt I was wearing that day, and to my utter shock there on my shirt was the number 15. I can't tell you how many times I've seen this photo over the last thirty-plus years, and I NEVER knew there was a number on my shirt—it just never caught my attention. Of all the numbers that my father-in-law could have chosen for my son, he chose the same number I had on my shirt when I was ten years old. This has been such a gift to my family—almost as good as seeing my son again (almost). We all healed a little from these signs, and there are more, but those two stand out to me, and I thought I should share them.

In memory of Bryant Graham

Author

Here is a nice example of how spirit is using newer technology like the GPS. They will adapt their delivery of signs to incorporate modern devices as well as using older, more recognized methods. Another example of a literal sign!

After being asked for a sign, Bryant decided to choose a very specific sign that would be connected to his dad. The sharing of the same number on go-karts decades apart was not only a personal sign but also a sign that reinforced the lasting bond between a father and son.

Section V

Transitioning

"Trust your life has meaning and it will be revealed to you when the time is right."

J.M.Higgins

Illness

Joe, this particular subject matter that you wanted us to discuss with you concerns the impact on the physical body of disease and other influences that can cause a breakdown of the physical structure.

We had talked about exit points and life plans earlier in the book, and this would be a good time to give you some examples of how those subjects play out.

When the life plan is being organized, there are certain occasions that can be preplanned into one's life that will create opportunities for learning. During the preplanning stage, certain events can be altered, and an individual's free will may change the direction of their life path.

So, when it comes to an illness or a physical deterioration of the human body, we can use those opportunities to learn various lessons. I know you like to use the phrase "pencil in," and to a certain extent this is true. The fact that an individual can change the lesson plans allows possible growing experiences to be achieved in their life.

By this, we mean that an illness can be preplanned for certain experiences and lessons, and it can also be preplanned to be a flexible opportunity that can be utilized if needed. An illness or physical change to the body can allow the individual to use their free will while still having certain opportunities available. For instance, a particular illness that has been preplanned may not be necessary at a particular time, as the lessons and knowledge that were sought have already been acquired, and therefore the opportunity available through the illness is no longer needed.

At other times, the soul may decide at a particular time that an illness would be a great facilitator to bring about the opportunities that it seeks.

The illness itself can vary, depending on the degree of experience and knowledge that need to be acquired. Sometimes the illness can be used as an exit point after the individual has acquiring all the needed experiences they wished to accomplish in this lifetime.

Other times, an illness may be used for its potential as a growing experience for others around that particular individual. Illness is a broad term that can affect not only the person but many other people associated with that person. It has the ability to affect others very slightly or to a higher degree. This all depends on the interactions between the individual and the other souls who are in alignment with them.

So, the opportunity for growth through a particular illness has many facets to it and can be moved around within one's life span. A particular event that may have been preplanned to play out in someone's twenties may not be necessary and may be restaged at a later time in one's life. Even then, when the illness does play out, it might not be to the extent that it would have been if it had taken place earlier in the life cycle.

So, when the soul is preplanning some of the opportunities it wishes to create on the Earth plane, an illness creates a very flexible situation that can be moved around from one age to another, from one degree to another, and from one length to another. This flexibility can create multiple opportunities not only for the individual but also for the other souls who have accompanied the person for this particular life cycle.

Author

I have personally witnessed this in someone's life. A woman lost her daughter, and her other child was beginning to have some medical issues. After being asked to "check in" to see if I could give any insights, I was made aware of the severity of those issues. The woman and her daughter did not have any awareness of the severity of the medical condition.

I had a lot of questions concerning this particular situation, and I needed to seek out some understanding as to why this situation was playing out before I was ready to tell the mother what I had received. I encourage the mother to seek medical attention for the daughter as soon as possible without sharing the burden with her that she might lose her second child. While seeking out some of the answers to this particular situation, I was informed that this particular illness did not have to play out to the degree that I had been shown.

When I asked why, I was told it was not necessary for the mother to lose her second child because of the circumstances that had surrounded the loss of her other daughter. The other daughter had used an exit point for her transition. But to the parents, it was still the loss of a loved one. So, everything that was experienced had already taken place and did not need to be repeated. Therefore, the other child's medical condition became benign, and there was no reason to inform them as to the new outcome. I didn't want to bring unnecessary anguish to the family, as it was not necessary. I was told later by the mother that the daughter was fine and only needed a minor procedure.

How does that play out when someone loses more than one child, I asked?

Under these particular circumstances when more than one child passes, it is the understanding of the children to play out these opportunities in tandem. And when we say together, the souls of the children work together on a soul level in creating the situation. It is something that has been organized and drawn out before their arrival.

We understand that it is very difficult to comprehend the loss of a child, let alone the loss of multiple children. But this is exactly why we have been giving you this knowledge—so you can see the insights that are at play in the background. These are not just random events; there is a connection on the soul level between multiple souls, including the parents at certain times, even though they may not understand it while living out the actual events as they happen.

Everything else takes place as it should, meaning there are guides and loved ones, and many are involved in this particular type of situation. Much growth can be attained when this plays out, and the opportunities are created far and wide for others to achieve some of their goals. We don't wish to create despair; we wish to enlighten you that the children have more control of the situation than you believe. It is playing out as it was meant to in most of these instances. Some instances may be acts of free will in joining a friend or sibling in a crossing event, but those, too, have been preplanned to a certain extent. How and whether they were to play out depends on a soul's free will in deciding whether to take this opportunity at a particular time.

Illness can also become a factor in other methods of transitioning. Illness has many avenues it can take in order to create the lessons that others seek. Someone may have one illness, while another may have many. Some will regain their health very quickly, and for others it may cause their transition back to our side.

It is all very flexible, as we said before, and this is why it is considered a "moving "opportunity, meaning it can be moved around to different times in one's life span.

So, Joe, illness can be used by the soul to have flexibility in its preplanning of opportunities and lessons. It can be expanded and retracted to the degree that is needed during an individual's lifetime. A soul will use its free will to determine what level of illness will happen.

Straightforward preplanning illness events are also quite common. These are major events that are the reason for coming to the Earth plane. And as we mentioned earlier, illness can also be used as an exit point, and this, too, takes place frequently.

So, we wish for all to understand that there are other things at play when it comes to illness and the human body. The soul uses these opportunities to create events that may not have played out at a particular time. It may seem counterproductive to be willing to experience an illness when one is trying to live their life to the fullest. But, in fact, illness is a major facilitator for growth and learning.

Violence & the Passing of a Child

It is often very difficult for a parent or anyone who loses a child to understand the concept of a transition when it is surrounded by violence. To watch a human who was in a vulnerable state, such as a child, be involved in a violent event can cause trauma, disillusionment, and hopelessness for those dealing with the situation.

It is our intention to bring hope to those who have been affected by this manner of passing. At times, some of this information will not be accepted as true, and other times people will accept this information, as it comes from a place of love.

It is not our intention to create disillusionment or to bring any disharmony to an individual. We are here to help in the healing process individuals will go through when a child transitions from your side back to ours.

During the transition of a child as a result of a violent event, certain circumstances take place prior to the passing as well as directly afterward. Preparations are made as the event is occurring in order to release the soul from the human body. It is in this time frame that the soul will retract from the human body as the physical act of violence is occurring. Those involved in this incident are unaware of this procedure happening. By this, we mean that the child may not be aware that their soul is preparing to leave their body. On a deeper level, they are already connected to their loved ones on the other side. Those who are ready to greet the soul have prepared to be available for this transition. They have been notified by the soul of the child about the incident through a series of connections that we all share between the two sides.

It may sound as if this transition has been planned in advance, and sometimes this may be true. However, most often it is a random act of violence due to the corruption of one's life plan choices. There is constant communication between your side and our side on the physical, emotional, and spiritual levels. At any time, these lines of communication can open and transfer knowledge and information from your side to ours or from our side to yours. In the event of a tragic passing, the lines of communication are open from your side back to ours. It is at this time that those who will be needed to accept the soul's return are organized and placed in a position to greet the child.

We understand that some people might not be able to accept this information as it is intended. That is because all of you are at different levels of understanding and growth. So, we will try to explain this information as basically as possible, as it can become complex on many different levels. We don't want to confuse people as to how an event plays out, so we are trying to describe it in as simple a manner as possible.

When this transition occurs, the child's soul will leave the human body and will be accepted and greeted by those who have been chosen to work with this particular individual. They have agreed to guide this individual during its tenure on the Earth plane. Some may accept this as a guardian angel or as family guides who have taken on the responsibility to oversee the learning experience of that individual.

The main idea we wish to pass along is that the child is never alone during this transition. From the moment the decision has been made that a transfer will occur, the child is surrounded with loving support and compassion. This is true prior to the event, during the event, and then of course after the passing.

The child may appear to be physically suffering during a particular event in the passing; however, it is at peace in its internal structure and awareness of what is happening. Many times when you see a human suffering in their physical body, you assume they are suffering on many different levels. However, this is often not the case, and we see this in the passing of a child in a violent event. Their needs are met to the fullest, and the support surrounding them is of the highest degree.

The suffering you endure after losing a child is many times more painful than the actual passing of the child. Once the child is free of the human body, it is accepted into the loving world from which it came. It begins its transition process back to the spiritual realm and all that it offers to the growth of the soul.

In other words, the child is completing its process of returning to its original sphere of existence. The hardest part about that process is the experience of those left behind. The pain and suffering we can feel on our side resonates quite strongly for all those involved. These include guides, loved ones, and anyone associated with the child. We feel the anguish, terror, and sadness of those left behind, and oftentimes we need to intercede so others do not endure suffering that is not necessary.

We understand the grieving process on the Earth plane, and we support this natural way of interpreting a passing. However, at times we need to intercede so that others do not change their soul plan before it is carried out.

ALWAYS CONNECTED: FOR THOSE WHO HAVE LOST CHILDREN

At times when a child passes, the grief that takes place in the human body as well as the emotional body can cause unhealthy manifestations such as physical addictions, self-harm, and mental confusion. Other manifestations can also occur on the human level.

So, it needs to be stated that the passing of a child through a violent event can affect those left behind in such a way that could hurt their soul growth to the point where we must intercede so that they regain their balance in order to continue to grow. We work with the individuals who have suffered through the passing of a child in order to bring them healing and peace. This interaction can be ongoing for as long as necessary, and we continue to send love and surround those individuals with compassion and insights.

Oftentimes people will want to know whether the child suffered during the transition. The child is not capable of suffering through the transition, as the process is one of compassion, love, and understanding. The child's soul understands the process and is easily accepted back into the spirit realm. The child was not surprised or even curious as to what was happening, as they already know the procedure once it takes place.

When one comes to the Earth plane, certain information is registered within the soul that can be activated once the transition is about to occur. The human may not be aware of certain procedures and certain abilities that the soul has, but in fact was with the soul as it arrived on the Earth plane. It comes with many facets of information, insights, and abilities that are unknown to the human.

Some of these attributes have been discussed in the past, such as the abilities of laughter, kindness, and compassion, which can bring healing and health not only to those who receive it but also to those who give it. The so-called tools that have been brought with you from the other side.

One of those tools is the knowledge of soul transfer. A child of any age will have this information embedded in their soul so that when it is time for their crossing, they are fully aware of the procedure.

From the outside, a violent passing may seem as if the child has been ripped away from their loved ones unnecessarily and have suffered to an extent that is uncalled for. This, in fact, is true to a certain extent, as the means of passing can be traumatic to all left behind.

Traumatic transitions at any age will be looked at more harshly than a simple passing from old age. However, the procedures for transition are the same.

Physical suffering occurs in many different ways, and understanding it can be complex, to say the least. Any type of suffering is often looked upon as traumatic and uncalled for, especially when a child is involved, as it exaggerates the level of unease and difficulty.

All children who have passed through violent means will not affect how they're accepted on our side. Once the transition begins to occur, the love and compassion of our side intercede to the fullest. Before the transition begins, there are also interactions by our side in order to protect the child or loved one from accepting the circumstances they are currently going through. The confusion that a soul may take on during this process is of utmost importance to us so it does not slow the soul's progress once on the other side. We are aware of the physical process that is taking place and are actively supporting the child as it plays out.

The child—as well as an adult, for that matter—is never alone when going through an event such as this. The circumstances surrounding such a passing may cause it to seem as though the individual is isolated in their own fear and trauma. However, this does not affect the soul or the resulting transition.

We have the opportunity here to try to relieve some of the pain and misunderstanding surrounding the passing of a child as a result of a traumatic event. We want to be able to pass along the information that a child, even though young in human years, can still have the necessary tools to deal with such a tragic passing.

There are forces at play that shield the child from such a tragic passing. Oftentimes the child will not recognize the passing as dramatic, as those left behind will. The child will understand the circumstances surrounding the passing much better than those on the Earth plane. They have much more insight and understanding into the complexities of the particular event.

The adults who are left behind will search for answers that they are not capable of understanding. This constant search can bring harm and unease to the physical body. The child can observe this from the other side and often wishes to intercede to bring comfort and support to those left behind. They will use multiple ways to try to connect to those left behind in order to let them know that they are pain-free, not suffering, and are surrounded by loving friends and guides.

They feel the grief of those left behind and are aware that such a tragic passing will affect those close to them. They want those left behind to understand that they wish their loved ones to be free of the intense grief that they are currently experiencing.

The more traumatic the passing, the more love the child will try to send back to the Earth plane. This can be done through memories, laughter, and even signs at the proper time.

The passing of a child, no matter the manner, will bring trauma and suffering to those left behind. If it is through a violent act, family members, friends, loved ones, and anyone else involved will perceive the crossing to be much harder than if the child had passed in another manner. In fact, this is not true. The transition will be the same, as the manner in which the body has ceased to exist does not equate with a more traumatic crossing.

At times people believe that a violent crossing, such as through an auto accident, traumatizes the soul when it leaves the body. This could be true for child or an adult, but this is not always the case. Many times when a transition happens quickly, the soul has already left the body and is quite aware of its surroundings and loved ones nearby.

If an older child or even an adult passes quickly and is somehow shocked as to their new surroundings, it is because they have become acutely aware that the physical limitations of the Earth plane are no longer relevant. However, they're also aware of the loving greeting that is taking place. So in truth, sometimes the soul is abruptly aware of the new surroundings, but it is not lost or stuck in some translucent world. The soul's natural ability to find its way home is triggered, no matter the situation, and those who are believed to be stuck are in essence not.

On the Earth plane, many people equate a tragic, violent passing with a more difficult transition. This is not the case—we do not allow this to happen, and it is not part of the complexities of being born and transitioning back to the spiritual plane.

Murder

Joe, we realize that the subject of murder is a very difficult topic for individuals on your side to understand. It is complex, to a certain degree, and explaining it will take some time. Often there are other life plans playing out in conjunction with this event. By this, we mean that there are other people experiencing certain events in their life that may coincide with the act of murder. These interactions can be on many different levels, such as health workers, law enforcement, and others related to that particular situation.

We have been asked if the act of murder is a preplanned event for those involved. Our answer is that no preplanning of this nature would involve an event such as murder. It is one type of event that occurs randomly, and when it does happen, others' life plans are disrupted. Many life experiences and growth opportunities will come out of such an event, but it is only after the event has played out that these opportunities are available. Oftentimes people have major growth spurts after dealing with a tragic event such as murder. Some people may become more outspoken for victims' rights, enter the medical field as a way of helping children, or simply realize the importance of life itself and how it should be cherished every day.

There are times when the passing of many through a violent act can be attributed to the definition of murder. Many souls crossing over at the same time because of an act of violence associated with murder can happen as a preplanned event. In this circumstance, a special association exists among the members of the group to exit the Earth plane together and to create life experiences for those left behind as well as for their own soul growth. This can happen when a group of souls decides that a particular event would be the best way to achieve this growth. You see this under categories such as genocide, the Holocaust, or any group that has a common theme and that passes dramatically.

Some large groups will also use naturally occurring events such as earthquakes, tsunamis, drought, and other situations to pass over as a group.

It also should be noted that the actions of war are complex and play out differently from individuals involved in murder within civilian life.

However, those are group situations, and they are more complex than individuals passing due to a violent event such as murder. The individual act itself is not the learning experience—it is the consequences of such an action that can lead to positive soul growth for many different people.

Adult children can initiate the circumstances around a murder to a certain degree. By this, we mean they are aware of the situations that they are involved in on a soul level. They understand that their interaction with certain individuals may corrupt their life's plan. They realize that taking a chance and discovering new avenues of learning can at times lead to their early transition back to the spirit realm.

Joe, by this we mean that children and younger individuals may seem naïve around certain violent acts, but their understanding of it is much deeper. Your perception of this type of interaction is difficult to understand, and we realize that many of your readers will have a difficult time understanding this. But what we wish to convey is that when an individual passes as a result of the act of murder, they are not harmed on the soul level at all. In actuality, the soul takes a big leap in development for having been involved in the situation because the soul can see the perspectives of all those involved. Not only does it see its own perspective but also the perspective of the person or persons who are causing this act.

The soul also has the perspective of seeing the circumstances surrounding that particular event. Sometimes the surroundings may indeed influence the act of murder that otherwise might not have played out at that time or place. But the child has access to this insight, and from that its learning opportunities are magnified due to the circumstances surrounding the violent transition.

Children who have passed from this act can teach others who transition before their time about accepting the achievements they have made on the Earth plane. These children have special insight that will be very healing to others who transition and who might need extra care.

It's as if they get a promotion by going through such an event. They will have the opportunity if and when they return to the Earth plane to be of service to others who have lost a child in a similar manner. Oftentimes counselors, therapists, law enforcement, and healthcare workers have been victims of murder in the past. Upon returning to the Earth plane, they have brought this insight deep into their soul and are able to help those who are experiencing the effects of a murder.

We realize that some people might misinterpret this as us saying that all health workers or counselors have been murdered in a past life. This is not the case, but there are some who have decided to return to the Earth plane in order to bring peace and comfort to those who may be involved in the act of murder. Their insights and compassion will help those who suffer from the loss of a loved one through this manner.

This is an example how the complexities of certain crossings can create events and opportunities for growth on both sides of the veil. What comes out of a violent random act becomes a huge growth opportunity for many souls who are intertwined with the event.

We realize how difficult it is to understand such a tragic transition, and we understand that your perceptions on the subject are limited. So we wanted to give you some details about what happens or what is possible during such an event.

Joe wants to ask us how the parents of murdered children can understand even the possibility of such a crossing.

It is best for you to remember that each individual soul, when it comes to the Earth plane, has the ability to change its direction, change its path, and accept new learning opportunities. At times, some of the decisions that are made will not play out as intended. The interference that can be caused by mutual individuals who decide to abandon their original path can coincide in violent acts, of which murder is just one. These individuals may have had circumstances around their life path that did not play out as anticipated and may have decided to seek a totally different direction. This is not totally uncommon and can be seen in some individuals who turn their life around after having a difficult start.

But as events play out and situations are co-created differently from their original intentions, certain events will come into play. An example of such events may be the destruction of an airplane by someone who intended it to crash. It may play out on an individual or group basis.

The complexities of the interplay of the souls in such events are layered and somewhat complex. For the purpose of this book, we do not wish to explain all these different avenues, for it could be a book in itself. What we do wish to convey is the concerns people have around the circumstances of the murder of a child.

We do not want to make it overbearingly complex, even though there is much at play.

The child's soul during this particular event is surrounded within an energy of love and compassion that shields its essence from the act itself. Its physical body may show emotion and distress, but the consciousness and soul of the child are free from the act. They are protected and often become the lead observer of these events. By this, we mean that since certain events happen to everyone on the Earth plane, you are always surrounded by guides and loved ones, and they can observe the ups and downs of your daily life. When a child passes as a result of this violent means, they are often the lead observer gaining the insights and understanding at a higher level than many of the other witnesses. They truly are an enlightened soul for going through such an event. This soul in essence burns very strongly on our side. People who have transitioned from this act become strong leaders and teachers for having done so. They are admired for their growth.

Those individuals who commit a murder could have had their own life plan corrupted enough to be at the point of being involved in such an act. There are different levels of corruption; some may occur naturally, like not knowing how to deal with anger, jealousy, or greed, while others will come from outside influences such as the misuse of alcohol or drugs.

Once this take place, the individual blocks out their natural tools to help guide them in their decision-making process. The human being is now totally relying on its *physiological* makeup to provide the guidance in the situation. So, instead of having access to higher insights that each individual naturally comes to the Earth plane with, the individual will rely only on their human makeup and will try to resolve perceived problems in as easy a way as possible.

Evil

There are occasions when the victim will come into contact with individuals who do not have the same type of essence as those who come from our side. They do not come from a place of love and therefore will exhibit actions that are void of any compassion or kindness.

These individuals are created directly from a source consisting of anger, anxiety, fear, and extreme cruelty. These entities manifest into physical form using the energy created by the above emotions.

These entities are not intended to be constructive or to have a particular life purpose. They're created with only one intent, and that is to create consistent fear and anger, and to terrorize. Their eternal makeup consists of these facets, and they are allowed to take human form by the mere fact that they have access to your plane of existence. These "soulless" individuals are repulsed by compassion and good. Their anger feeds their soul and is the energy they thrive on. It corrupts the human body condition, and in order for it to thrive, it will continue with these acts in order to sustain itself on the Earth plane.

Some of these individuals are highly intelligent and can dissuade others from believing who they really are. They have the ability to morph and to appear similar to others while hiding their deeper self-turmoil.

Dealing with these individuals

It is difficult to comprehend the depth of their darkness when we try to explain how they become. There are levels of depravity that are far deeper and darker than you can conceive. It is not that we are trying to frighten you—we are just allowing you the knowledge that there are these entities who have access to the Earth plane. They come in different situations and can be disguised as popular people, friends, and even loved ones. You might see this in a child serial killer who is married and is respected in their profession.

If you feel very uncomfortable around a particular individual, it is possible that they may be one of these entities. We understand your concern about wanting to identify these entities without having to examine all your connections on the Earth plane.

Your internal compass is the true measure of whether you are in the presence of one of these evil individuals. They can hide their outward appearance and disguise their actions in various situations; however, it is difficult for them to hide their interior motives and their makeup. It is this that makes them recognizable. This is how they can be exposed. You have the ability, all of you, to expose these individual entities if you learn the technique that we are about to mention to you.

If you are in a situation where you believe that an entity of this composition is in your environment, you may seek out ways in order to identify them. One of the ways is to rely on your basic instincts. This is the fundamental way each individual can test a certain situation and other individuals to see if they are in proper alignment. So, we wish you to use your "gut instinct" in order to investigate the situation.

Another method is to ask others how they are feeling concerning a certain person or situation. If there is agreement around a group of you that something is amiss, this is also a way of telling if there is an outside influence in this particular situation. Some of you may doubt your gut instinct, but when it is measured against others and you see that they are similar, you will understand that your initial feelings were correct.

One way we have found to work in exposing these type of entities is to remember that love is stronger than the brightest star in the sky. *The power of love can delve deep into the existence of any entity that is allowed on the Earth plane.* Focusing love and compassion at a particular entity will weaken them as well as what feeds them, which is fear and anxiety. By applying compassion and love to the situation, things begin to manifest that change the makeup of these individuals as well as situations that all are involved in.

When love is implemented toward these entities, they withdraw into themselves and begin to question their actual being. *It may not be noticeable on the surface, but the power of love can penetrate to the deepest, darkest regions of existence.*

So we ask that you not only surround yourselves with love but also radiate it out to others who may be affected by these individuals. Direct application of loving guidance, compassion, and thoughtfulness toward the individual entity will make them helpless and unable to carry out their misdeeds.

Author

I ask this question because it relates to the abuse and killing of children during periods of genocide and the Holocaust.

How does this work on a larger scale?

In this particular situation, as with others you will study or have studied, there will always be a group of individuals who are controlled and eventually killed by these entities.

The entities attempt to destroy the physical manifestation you call the body while not understanding that they cannot touch the soul of those they have persecuted. They attempt to bring as much suffering as possible to the Earth plane as that is where they are attached to. Once a person has passed and the soul retracts from the body, they are no longer held captive by these entities.

As for applying love to the situation to dissipate those individual spirits, what we have seen in history is that others rise up to overcome these individuals. The individuals are overwhelmed by the majority of people—individual souls banding together—who pray for their destruction and send love to those who have been restrained by these entities.

Even in the midst of chaos, war, and other destruction, there is a constant flow of love throughout them. This love can be found individually as well as through groups. This loving energy creates turmoil in the chaos and begins to return it to its normal flow. To the observer, it may seem as if no action has taken place, but on the sub level, the influence of the love energy creates the turning point when the righteousness eventually conquers the evil force.

Joe, this is why the power of prayer individually and in groups is so important. It can radiate out among chaos and destruction and create new waves of energy that begin to turn the tide and bring hope and eventually peace.

It is one of the most powerful tools that you as individuals and as group of individuals have in determining your growth and support the process of helping each other. Someone witnessing this can call it miracles or the winning of the war. It can happen on a small scale with individuals or a large scale, such as a world war.

To create this wonderful, powerful energy, one only needs to sit quietly and asked that their thoughts merge with others who wish to bring compassion and love to a particular situation. This allows the energy to more quickly be created for that particular reason. It forms a conduit for the energy to be focused on that particular situation. The more this is utilized, the more peace can be created on your Earth plane.

Addictions

Unfortunately, people often seek out a release from the stress of everyday life that may be caused by a physical ailment or a psychological situation the individual is trying to deal with. The cause of the stress can be complex or simple. A simple cause could be a recent event or a misunderstanding concerning themselves. A more complex situation could be something that happened many years prior or with others who may have interacted with this individual in a way that caused a long-term psychological issue.

When an individual becomes actively involved in trying to re-enact a physical or mental sensation, this is considered an addiction. However, many times the reenactment will not match the previous experience. At these times, the individual's mind will try to control the outcome of their actions. By this, we mean that if someone is addicted to a *physical* substance, and if adding or taking away that substance can cause relief or pain, the mind will try to figure out the best way to get the body into balance and bring relief.

Oftentimes people who are addicted to certain behaviors, medication, or thought patterns do so in hiding—out of sight of friends and family. This in itself adds to the problem. As an individual becomes more isolated in their addiction, the addiction takes on more power to control the individual on a soul level. By this, we mean that as someone begins to succumb to the activities of addiction, they increasingly give up control of the connection to their true self. They become separated from the tools and insights they have brought with them from our plane before their birth.

This search for any answers to the problems they are currently experiencing feeds the addiction cycle to the point of taking over the human experience. It begins to control their actions, thoughts, and goals. Life suddenly becomes centered on a particular addiction, which separates the individual from their life's path.

Not only do addictions affect the individuals who are caught up in them, but they can affect the life paths of others associated with the person. Family, friends, and other loved ones are all touched by an individual who has become actively involved in an addictive behavior. Their life paths can also be altered in order for this type of event to be incorporated into learning experiences for others who are in the situation. However, oftentimes plans will become corrupted, and the human mind will try to correct this corruption, causing a further imbalance and possibly leading to the passing of the individual.

We know that oftentimes people may experiment with illicit drugs or even prescription medications and cause their own transition by mistake. This act falls into the category of free will. Similarly, someone who is speeding in an unsafe setting is exercising their free will and may also cause their own transition.

Free will begins to be corrupted as the human body goes through physiological changes. Even if the individual sees what is happening to them, they are often unable to bring the body and mind back into balance with their inner self. As these events play out, despair, lack of hope, and depression often come into play.

Many individuals have come to the Earth plane with the idea that an addiction could be a path to learning. This is true, to a certain extent, and there are many who have taken this on in their life. It is a difficult path to take, and we support those who decide to take on this burden.

Sometimes the addiction is preplanned so the individual will have an opportunity to grow and understand the source. These actions can then be worked into a life plan in order to satisfy some of the goals the soul has set up before arriving on the Earth plane. We see this with people who have overcome their addictions enough to help not only themselves but also help many others achieve a healthy and peaceful life.

However, sometimes once an individual is in physical form, the addiction that may have been planned out in order to achieve certain goals begins to override the individual's senses and begins to disrupt their original reason for existing.

Other addictions can be implemented in an individual's life plan as they decide to join other soul groups to participate in some of the lessons they have planned out. You might see this in a person who has conquered their addiction and goes on to become a counselor to those who have lost control of the opportunity they originally thought they could handle.

So, there is a spiritual component to the activity of addictions as well as the aspect of falling into its grasp through free will. Some, but not all, people can relate to this aspect, as they have seen loved ones in this state of being.

Other times, people cannot understand the concept of an addiction and believe, wrongly, that it's something that can simply be controlled. There is more at play here, and having such a limited understanding is not a compassionate way to deal with the situation.

We can help many of those who wish to have an intervention in order to help relieve the burden of the addictive activity. Children who have passed through this method will often assist those on the Earth plane who seek help in their fight to regain their original state of being. We wish to help people understand how addictive behavior can cause someone to lose their physical life. As we have seen many times when a younger person participates in an addictive action, it can cause distress to their body, both physically and mentally. We also see how an individual may try to change their actions to stop the ongoing addictions, but the physical and mental makeup of the body makes it most difficult. We see this when they are willing to take actions to stop the situation but are not successful due to being overridden by the brain trying to reenact what it was taught, which is to relieve pain and suffering.

One of the important things that we wish for your readers to understand is that a transition that results from some form of addiction is only a different way of passing. True, it seems as though there is more involvement by the individual than perhaps in an illness, but it's still the individual who decides to take part in the activity. Even if it's just through association with other soul groups, it's still a free will decision.

When a child passes because of addiction they have been involved in, they see their life from a different perspective and realize the control they thought they had was actually lost to the chemical and physiological changes that were happening in their physical body. They realize this and wish for those left behind to understand that they did not have the ability to deal with the situation on the physical plane. Other times, it may be simply an act of free will to partake in an activity that may cause the body to wish to reenact an event and therefore caused the transition of the child. We sometimes see this when someone overdoses on a particular drug they thought was not as powerful as they later realized.

We have asked some of the children to come through and give you some insights from their passing and to help alleviate some of the guilt and suffering parents feel when they have lost a child to an addiction.

Insights into Addiction

Those Who Have Passed Over Due to Addictions

Charles

Hi, Joe. My name is Charles, and I passed suddenly as a result of overdosing on medicine I was given for an injury I got from working out. The injury was minor, but things began to snowball after I started taking the painkillers. I realized their effect on me was more than just silencing my physical pain; they were also helping my mental pain.

It's not something you expect when you start down that road, but things take over after a while, and before you know it you're relying on this outside source to make you feel good. The intentions at the beginning were great for everyone concerned, and the medication was really helping me with my back pain and left leg pain. I decided to use the medication because I wanted to continue with my workouts, and otherwise I would have had to stop. My intention was to become stronger, but I didn't know that I needed to work on the inner me more than my physical body.

So, after a while I relied upon the medication to ease the burdens

I was going through at that time. I had doubts about myself, about my relationships, and about how I fit into the world. When I took the medication, it took the edge off of it and made me slightly numb to my surroundings and whether I belonged. Before long, it was a necessary part of my life; without the drugs, I couldn't handle my everyday life. Not only was there a physical withdrawal if I didn't take them but also a mental and emotional withdrawal.

I already had a problem dealing with others in my circle, and when I stopped taking the drugs, the problems escalated. My physical body ached without them, and I couldn't function physically or mentally unless I took more than had originally been prescribed.

After a while, people noticed that I had started to change. They noticed that my attitude toward things was different from before my injury, but actually it was different from before I started taking the drugs. I was more sensitive to things and became irritated much more easily. I used to lash out at people and fight with them about every little thing. This became a problem within my family and my relationships, as no one wanted to be around me when I was "high." They knew something was up, but they weren't sure what it was, and I wasn't going to volunteer anything because I wasn't exactly sure what was causing my change in attitude.

As many of you know, the physical and emotional changes that occur after becoming addicted to certain substances are difficult to deal with. However, abstaining from the addictive substance creates its own problems—problems people can't see and that many of us have to deal with on our own.

It's this isolation that becomes like a cocoon for our ability to live and function in the real world. People don't get it when we try to hide away, but what we're trying to do is shelter ourselves from the pain we have on many different levels. We are often ashamed of the position we have put ourselves in and how we are dealing with our loved ones, which we never would have considered before the addiction. Some of you will relate to this and will see it in your own children as well as your colleagues as they struggle with this physical and mental disease.

Many times people with an addiction want to get help, and some of us actually seek out help and begin to work within a program. However, sticking to such new guidelines is often very difficult because the inner work that needs to be done is lacking. The perspective we have of ourselves causes minor distractions in our daily lives to grow out of control and take over who we are. It's true when people say we never expected to grow up to be addicts. A combination of forces create the opportunity to become overwhelmed in life and open the door for the possibility of addiction to sneak in.

I know I speak for many kids over here who wish they could apologize to their parents, siblings, loved ones, and friends for how they treated them and for passing over before it was their time. Our intentions were not to end our lives by overdosing; the sedation of our feelings was the primary goal. The side effect was the disruption to the physical body that caused it to cease functioning. In other words, the side effect was our own death.

We take responsibility for what happened, and we can now see how things played out in that most of the time, we didn't have any control in the situation. Our lives were often in chaos before, and this added to the problems as things begin to cascade downhill.

Some of us accidentally overdosed and were not addicted to drugs at all. This is different from those of us who had an ongoing, day-to-day problem with substance abuse.

We welcome hearing our loved ones talk to us as we take responsibility for our passing and use this new perspective to help others on the Earth plane. We have the ability to send compassion and self-healing to those who are struggling with addiction right now. We can influence certain situations and help individuals see that there is outside help available to them and help them respond to positive feedback. We also have the ability to help an individual become aware of their lack of self-love and understanding of their feelings. We work with children and adults who have hidden themselves from society and who try to deal with their problems alone. These are the most fragile individuals, as they are isolated, and we surround them with love and special care. We help them seek out opportunities for healing and make them aware that other people are willing to sacrifice their time and be patient in order to help them.

Joe, we are not going to get into how a soul plan may be in effect during one of these transitions. There are times when an individual will accept this type of exit plan in order to fulfill certain obligations it had planned on carrying out. By this, we mean certain life lessons had already been completed, and it was not necessary to continue on the Earth plane. But these individuals have much more complex situations around them, and it would take much more to explain the many different avenues that are being played out. So I wanted to focus in on those of us who became addicted physically and mentally because of the lack of love we have for ourselves and how that situation caused us to eventually pass over.

As mentioned before, our actions or free will, as you say, can cause us to take a different direction in our lives. We have the ability to adapt, and sometimes we tend to take the easy road. These adaptations of our life paths can cause us to get into situations where events such as an early crossover can occur. It is not necessarily the fault of the individual or those surrounding them on the Earth plane; it may be playing out due to other circumstances happening at the same time.

Wendy

Hi, Joe. This is Wendy. I'm really excited to discuss with all of your readers about my addiction and those who are going through it now. We know what you're going through, and we know how difficult it is to realize that there is another solution to what you think are your problems. This is directed not only to individuals who are currently addicted to certain substances but also to parents who may have guilt about our passing. Many times we had no idea what the results of our actions would be—we just didn't always think ahead. Education is really helpful to many, as it opens up the thoughts of other possible ways around the addiction path. But not always—sometimes it's just life playing out, that's all. That sounds sad, and to a certain extent it is, but many things are going on that we don't know about when we are over there in the physical world.

Victor

This is Victor, who passed when he was twenty-two.

Hi, Joe. Thank you for letting me come through today. It's really important that we reach out to our parents and all those who have lost children because of addictions. What we see when we cross over is a lot different from what we see while living it.

I had trouble adjusting to my life generally, and as I got older, it became more difficult for me to socialize outside my small group of friends. I had anxiety and distrust for certain people, and it just snowballed out of control. I know this sounds weird, but I enjoyed taking my meds, as they allowed me to be more popular around others. They helped me cope with the doubts I had about myself. They gave me a boost of confidence that I thought I needed. But in actuality, I didn't need anything; I had it inside me already, but instead I looked for an outside source to bump me up.

I started doing drugs when I was in the tenth grade, and I continued doing them until I passed over from an overdose. A lot of times people think you died because you took too much, but it's not always like that. Sometimes it's the buildup in your system—the constantly trying to reach that level you reached before. That's when it gets tricky because your judgment deceives you, and you think it's safe and that you can get away with it one more time.

My parents were divorced at the time, and I got along with them pretty well, but there were times when I was all by myself, and this created more doubt for me. I not saying it's my parents' fault at all. It's just that that's how the situation was, and it kind of gave me the opportunity to seek out other avenues. I talk to other kids over here who went through the same things I did, and we want to let people on your side know that it's okay. We realize we didn't have the tools to deal with the situations when we were living with you. We understand why we did what we did. There is no blame—it's just how things played out, and sometimes we got caught up in our own world and didn't realize that there were other methods to help ourselves.

Mom, Dad, I just want to say hi and also to my little brother, Tim. Keep working hard. I got your back, and I'll be there for you for the rest of your life.

Okay, thanks again, Joe. It's great to be able to get this off my chest so that others can read a little bit of my story and can understand that we are not suffering over here. We're actually very in tune with what's going on on your side. Just reach out and say hello once in a while because we're still here, we can still hear you, and we like a funny joke once in a while, too.

Barbara

Joe, we now have Barbara. She was eighteen when she passed over from a drug overdose.

Hi, Joe. Thank you for letting me come through today. It's so fun and exciting to be able to come through and reach out to your readers and let them know that we're okay over here. And actually, "over here" is kind of right next to you. When I say "kind of," we're doing other stuff too, but it's as if we're in the same room with you. Unfortunately, I ended my life with drugs and alcohol. It's a long story that I won't get into, but the main point is to try to reach out to children before it becomes a problem. I'm not saying you should over watch your children every second, but ask them how they're doing—not necessarily about school or their studies, but rather about how they're feeling inside and how they feel about the obstacles they run into in their lives. Simple questions like this will allow kids to open up and tell you how they truly feel. We hide things pretty well but will open up if we're asked the right questions with the right intent. Don't worry, you don't have to interview us every time we come in the door—that would actually shut us down. But a sincere interest in how we're feeling goes a long way.

But make sure that whatever happens, you don't take it on yourself as something you didn't do. There is way too much guilt on your side. It rips people apart and is so unnecessary. We all have our concerns and troubles on your side, but they don't have to be self-inflicted. Give yourself a break; it's as if you're slapping yourself in the face sometimes.

Be kind to yourself and don't worry about how we're doing because we're all doing great. We help each other over here, and we help you guys a lot over there. Believe me, we have a lot of work to do, ha ha. But we enjoy doing this type of work—we get a lot out of it. You'd be surprised how many people we can touch in with whom we can help with simple things like self-confidence and happiness. So, don't think you have to figure everything out on your side. There's a lot of things that go into addictions and overcoming them. You are only aware of a few ways of dealing with them. Trust your gut instincts about situations and do the best you can and then let it go. The last thing we want to see on our side is our parents suffering because of our mistakes. That's like dying all over again and seeing the hurt we have brought to others because of our actions. But we realize we were not in control when these things happened. It's a circumstantial transition (how's that for a big phrase, ha ha). It basically means we crossed over because of the circumstances surrounding something we were doing. We love you all very much and like it when you talk about us and laugh a little bit more. It feels so joyous when you think about us and share a laugh. I love that!

Kevin

Joe, Kevin would like to come through and share some information about himself.

Hi, Joe. My name is Kevin. I passed when I was sixteen by self-inflicted drinking and driving. I had just learned how to drive, and I had been drinking from a younger age. When you put those two things together, you have a recipe for disaster, and I took up on that. My parents were so angry with me when I died that they couldn't understand how everything played out. They tried to figure out every possible situation and couldn't come to the conclusion that it was a combination of my addiction to alcohol and the fact that I had no basic experience behind the wheel.

I took my brother's car one night and went to pick up some friends. They were all excited that we were going to go out and hang. But we never got to do any of that because I decided to have a couple of drinks before I took the car. I thought I was fine but didn't realize that my altered state created an opportunity for me to lose my life. It was an accident. Pure and simple. However, if I had not been addicted to alcohol, who knows what would have happened. I meet a lot of kids over here who passed over from drinking and driving. A lot of people don't realize that many of them were addicted to alcohol. Sometimes they think it was one night of drinking, but in actuality they were addicted to the drug, and the driving was secondary. It's not something we're proud of, but we do understand everything about it now that we're over here—how it interacts with the human body and how our emotions get intertwined with the chemical reactions. It's complex but also simple in another way.

So just a shout-out to my mom, dad, and Sherry, who still thinks about me a lot. I love you guys, I'm here for you, and I just hope I can help some parents understand that it's not always how things appear to be. There can be a lot more involved in passing over from an addiction.

Joe, thanks for letting the children come through today. We understand that you were looking for some stories concerning addictions, and we wanted to add one about alcohol, as many times people forget that alcohol is easily available and is used at an early age in many cultures. Some people have a predisposition to the effects of that particular drug and should be aware that it can lead to a physiological addiction. This can alter an individual's life plan and make things more difficult to achieve and enjoy during their life.

Abortion & Miscarriage

When people decide to bring a baby into your world, the decision is made on multiple levels. It is a combination of the Earth parents deciding whether they wish to procreate or perhaps even whether an individual woman wishes to conceive at some point in her life. There are many reasons that the act of conception plays out, and we don't want to get into the social or interpersonal factors upon which some of these decisions are made, as it might take away from the subject matter at hand.

When a soul on our side decides it wants to incarnate on the Earth plane, it will decide what goals it wishes to achieve before it's born. These goals will be organized into a life plan for opportunities to become available in order for these goals to be met. At times, some of these opportunities may change as life develops on the Earth plane, and therefore the soul must adjust its wants and needs.

On occasion, as the soul is prepared to incarnate on the Earth plane through birth, it sometimes has second thoughts. By this, we mean sometimes the soul realizes that some of the opportunities that will be created for it will not be able to be achieved in the way they have been laid out. Some will realize that the birth will in effect not be the opportunity for growth that was first imagined.

During these times, it is necessary for the soul to cancel its birth to the Earth plane, and therefore it must cease the pregnancy at some point. This decision is made not only by the soul but also by others who helped prepared the soul for its incarnation. The opportunity for birth may reside with the parents, but the decision about the actual birth resides with the child. The child is the leading factor in the creation of life on the Earth plane. It is the soul who decides when and how it will incarnate, and it will also decide if that incarnation needs to be abruptly stopped or even terminated soon after birth.

The child may feel that the interactions with others on the Earth plane may stunt its growth opportunities throughout its life. It may realize that the effort put into a long life will not allow it to grow and achieve the goals that were originally set. It may decide to reorient the goals and opportunities and to incarnate at a different time with different individuals involved.

This stop in a pregnancy can be called a miscarriage or even an abortion. These two terms have different connotations, but the result is the same in that the soul's incarnation has been stopped.

The soul of the child may decide, along with input from others on our side, in which manner it wishes to end the pregnancy. Both actions will have growth opportunities for the people involved on the Earth plane. So, the decision is worked into the life paths of those involved. Some of these situations may have actually been created between souls before the parents were even born. The parents were to lose a child at birth in their life plan in order to achieve certain goals and understandings surrounding life itself.

When the child decides, along with its guides, to make this decision, it will decide what opportunities are available to the parents in their life plans. The child will not wish to disrupt the plans that the adults have already put into place. So, opportunities will be sought out for the proper time and place and manner in which the pregnancy will end.

The soul does not necessarily connect with the physical child at birth. Sometimes the connection is made during the pregnancy and at other times after the physical birth has taken place. It depends on the soul of the child and how far they have determined to move into the Earth plane's existence.

When a miscarriage takes place, a complex series of events are taking place on our side that will play out in ending the pregnancy for reasons that the mother may not understand.

In the case of abortion, this particular act may be carried out for various reasons. In some cases, it will be worked into the woman's life plan and creates opportunities for growth and understanding, while in other cases it will create new opportunities for those around the situation to learn from. Remember, the decision to terminate the pregnancy has already been made by the child while on our side. It's just the manner in which the pregnancy terminates that can cause different opportunities for those on the Earth plane. From our perspective, there is no difference between the termination of the pregnancy through miscarriage or abortion. However, we do realize the social aspects of how things play out when one or the other method takes place. Some cultures looked down on women who have miscarriages, while other cultures actually persecute women who attempt an abortion. These are Earth-level judgments and understandings. They have nothing to do with the spiritual makeup of a child/parent coexistence. Oftentimes the mother may be thrust into turmoil and even guilt concerning one or the other of these methods, even though she has not been consulted about this event in the first place.

So, we want your readers to understand that there should be no shame or guilt with the ending of a pregnancy. There are reasons at play that neither the mother nor society realizes at that particular time. We do not wish to bring harm or unease to the mother or those surrounding and supporting her, but oftentimes this unease is created by those people themselves. People need to accept that there are more complex issues at play concerning bringing a soul into the Earth dimension. Parents and society often only see one perspective, and in many cases that perspective does not do the issue justice.

Take the time to enjoy the creation of a new physical being and the opportunities that come with that, but also understand that the opposite is true as well. Take the opportunities that have been presented by the ending of a pregnancy and use them to learn about compassion and love.

Sign Stories

A Literal Sign

I had asked my daughter, Jennifer, to send me a sign that she was still around and in my life. Nothing happened. A couple of days later, I attended a meeting of my professional women's organization. At the back of the room, we have a table where members can display their wares. A new member had some smallish wooden signs that she'd painted. One of them said "Mermaid Crossing." Thinking that Jen loved mermaids, I bought it.

When I got home, it occurred to me that not only had she sent me a literal sign (!), but the words "Mermaid CROSSING" were completely relevant. Duh! But that's not all... I emailed the woman who had painted the sign. She emailed right back and said she had goosebumps... she had been in her car, ready to go to the meeting, when she remembered she had wanted to bring some earrings to display. She went back in the house to get them and, on the way out, passed her worktable where she'd left the wooden signs she'd been working on that day. "For some reason," she decided to take the mermaid sign to the meeting.

Sheila Lowe, in memory of Jennifer Lowe

Author

At times we ask for a sign, but due to our busy lives we might end up missing it and wonder why. So sometimes they will be creative and use humor. The fact that the woman who painted the signs went back for earrings, only to see the mermaid sign sitting there, was all crafted by Jennifer to make sure her mom received what she'd ask for. She got a literal sign!

Feathers & a Birthday

I lost my son, Sven, in November 2016. He was just thirty-three, married, with three beautiful young children. After Sven died, I started to find small white feathers. They would suddenly show up in the most unexpected places, landing at my feet. From the very first feather, I knew it was him. It was his way of letting me know that he was around. Over and over, I was surprised by the unlikely prospect of a feather appearing, and then it did. One time, in the middle of the night, a single feather floated down from the ceiling in a closed room and landed at my feet. Another time, after sweeping the floor vigorously two times, returning the broom to the cupboard, and stepping back into the cleared space, there it lay — a single white feather that was not there a moment before. Each find makes my heart sing. I feel an overwhelming sense of gratitude and a deep joy.

ALWAYS CONNECTED: FOR THOSE WHO HAVE LOST CHILDREN

I celebrated a birthday in February this year, three months after Sven died. I was visiting my family in Johannesburg, almost 2000 kilometers from where we live. That particular morning I was to visit my sister, who is a beauty therapist, for some spoiling treatments. Her birthday gift to me was a small silver feather on a silk thread bracelet. It needed adjusting, and we decided to return to the store to see whether they could help. On the way there, my sister stopped off at her local coffee shop for her usual daily frappé. I had never been there before but chose to wait in the car while she collected the coffees. After a couple of minutes she came out, holding a bunch of seven white roses, tears in her eyes. "I think these are for you," she said. Attached to the roses was a printed card that read "Seven from Heaven," and the stem of one of the roses happened to cover the first *e*, so what I saw was "Sven from Heaven." Attached to the card was a single white feather. I immediately burst into tears and asked her where they had come from. She related that when she went into the coffee shop, the barista said that there was something that had been left for her and that she would know who they were for. Not he nor anyone else could remember who had brought them in. They assured us it was not any of her family. I had never been there before, and no one I knew would even know I would be there. In fact, we had just made the decision to return to the gift shop a short while before. This outing was not planned. There was no logical explanation. White roses, my favorite flowers. Seven, my favorite and special number, which also happened to be Sven's nickname when he was little. "Sven from Heaven," a white feather. Who could have orchestrated such a thing? Only my boy. He reached through the veil and delivered my most special birthday gift. There is no other way to understand this—no other explanation.

He continues to leave signs for me wherever I go. Last week, on the first day of my grief ceremony on the beach, the way was strewn with white feathers. The sea washed white feathers to my feet. They led me over the sand dunes and back to the lagoon. In the closing ceremony, there was a single white feather waiting for me in the sand. How can I ever doubt that he is here with me? In my darkest moments, there is always a light shining—the light of his love.

Laina, in memory of Sven

Author

These are two great sign stories with a special-occasion connection. Many times on special occasions, our loved ones wish to try to send a sign, as they know we are thinking of them. Our thoughts of them are an invitation to connect. In this case, Sven use a familiar sign that had been recognized in the past. Repeating the same type of sign makes it easier for them to send the sign, as less energy is need to complete the task. The fact that one of the stems was blocking the second letter shows how they can manipulate these types of events. It's not unusual for people to not be able to remember who had ordered or paid for gifts. There seems to be a piece of time that is blocked from people's memory. Strangers have been known to appear to carry out various roles, and then the details of their activities are quickly forgotten by anyone present. We refer to them as angels.

Blue Bird

Our sixteen-year-old son Bryan was murdered on 12/22/12. As you can imagine, it was a very painful time in our lives, including fears about whether Bryan had crossed over or was stuck in some kind of limbo because of such a sudden, tragic death. A month after his passing, his father, William, was working at a construction site when a blue bird came hopping straight toward him. He was standing with several other workers who were all in shock when they saw this bird just hopping toward William. He thought the bird may have been injured, so he bent down to pick it up. The bird calmly just let him hold it while William examined its wings. Everything looked fine, so he put the bird on the branch of a nearby tree and proceeded to get into his truck. The bird flew off the branch and straight into the truck. William picked up the bird and put it on his dashboard and just sat there watching the bird for a while. He took pictures and made a call to me, explaining what a strange thing was happening to him. After a little while, the bird just flew out the window. It was a beautiful sign our son Bryan sent to his dad so he could know he was fine. The bird wanted to be with William. It was a beautiful thing.

In memory of our son Bryan

Author

Bryan was definitely not in some "limbo." Even in cases of sudden, tragic deaths like Bryan's, they are greeted with much love on the other side. Your story brought a tear to my eye, as it was a great example of how they can use an animal to convey a sign and show how we are always connected. The fact that others witnessed the bird's behavior shows how when a group sign is used, it can magnify the connection. The others will also gain peace and insight by witnessing this event as they share that memory among themselves and remember it when they lose a loved one.

Still Taking Care

Here is a tiny, but for me powerful, sign I received from my son Sean.

I have a beautiful tree in my backyard that flowers every spring. Sean always trimmed that tree for me, and he was very proud of his work. (He was only nineteen when he passed, so using a chain saw was something he was just developing skill with.) Two years ago, the Cape was hit with very high winds, snow, and sleet. Another tree fell on top of my flowering tree, and both trees had to be cut down. I was heartbroken because I loved the tree. Just the stump was left, but I noticed that the tree grew new branches and flowered this spring! Spirit is always with us, and I always need those messages!

In memory of my wonderful son, Sean Stigberg-Mellman

Author
Sean knew how important that tree was to his mom, and he had a shared interest in it as well. A shared interest is a wonderful way to send a sign, as the connection to the loved one is already there. It's just a matter of realizing that the loving connection still exists.

Every Night

In 2014, my family life went through some changes, and I began to miss my sister a great deal. Once more, I tirelessly asked for signs during this time. I recall that every night, my closet door would open while I slept. Even if I woke up in the morning and closed it, I would wake up to it open nightly. I began hearing my sister's voice in between dreams, as well as music we both enjoyed listening to while she was still here.

In memory of Karla

Author

Dreams are the easiest way for our loved ones to connect with us. Our attention to daily life has been reduced, and the sleep state makes the transfer of information more adaptable. Karla not only slipped in her voice between dreams but reinforced it with music they both had enjoyed. Once again, loved ones often pick out a shared memory so as to stand out from other random stimuli.

The Word, Not The Sound

I was waking up one morning and was in a drowsy state as I was coming out of sleep. I felt this great puff of wind go by my right ear. I was lying face down, which isn't easy for me, and I heard the word *ka-boom*. That's what struck me at first. I remember my first instinct was that my angel was learning to fly and she crashed on the roof. But it was the word *ka-boom* as opposed to the sound of an explosion. So I immediately bolted up and in doing so, I woke the dogs, who were sleeping on the bed. If they had heard a real explosion, they would have been up and off the bed before I had even realized anything. That was an interesting way for Emma to get my attention.

Karyn, in memory of Emma

Author

By Emma using the word ka-boom *instead of an actual sound, her mom noticed the difference as something particular. If it had been a real explosion or loud noise, she might not have made the connection. But Emma knew her mom and picked the right manner to send the successful sign.*

My Beautiful Butterfly

I always called my beautiful, spirited granddaughter "my beautiful butterfly waiting for a place to land." A few weeks after her passing, when I was at her grave, a beautiful butterfly landed next to my foot. It stayed there a long time. I didn't move, as I didn't want the butterfly to fly away. It flew away but came back, this time landing on the area where she is buried. The grass hadn't grown in yet, and the butterfly hovered over the area and kept lifting up and touching down over the entire burial site. After a while, it flew away again, and I still couldn't leave. It came back, landed on the headstone, and then flew to the next headstone and the next one. I followed it. Then it flew to and around my car and disappeared. My beautiful butterfly was telling me she found her place to land and led me to my car to say it was okay for me to go home.

I also had a dream about my granddaughter very soon after

her parting. In the dream, she appeared in an informal garden. She looked the way she did when she was ten years old and was wearing the same white dress she had worn for a special occasion. She had a beautiful, peaceful look on her face. Not long after that, I had another visitation dream. It was just her face. It was in black and white, and she was surrounded, as if she were in the center of a wreath, by many, many young faces. They were all smiling, and their faces were in sepia tones. I had this exact dream three times.

In memory of Erin Noble

Author

When you mention "led me to my car to say it was okay for me to go home," I think your granddaughter was trying to say that she was going home with you — that she would be with you always.

In the second story, you mention "she was surrounded, as if she were in the center of a wreath, by many, many young faces. They were all smiling." This was to show that they are not alone on the other side. Many times, children come through with other kids around them.

Section VI

Signs

"When you accept a sign from our side you are actually affirming your own true existence as a beautiful spirit that learns that there is no death."

J.M.Higgins

The Language

❧

When a child is first born and is learning to communicate, you have to learn a whole new way of interacting with this new being. No baby is born talking multiple languages, knowing what symbols mean, and understanding the concepts of interpersonal relationships. They learn these things as they grow. So, now it is your turn to learn these new communication methods after a child has passed.

What Are Signs?

"Signs are a method we use to communicate from our side, or what you might call the afterlife, to your side. At times we have attempted to communicate through other methods, some of which were successful, while others were a total disappointment. An example of one of the other methods of communicating with you was through the use of astrology, or the alignment of certain heavenly bodies surrounding your planet. Some of these techniques are used today but not as they were originally intended.

That particular method was misunderstood, as it was interpreted by individuals who were not those to whom the signs were directed. Often what happens is that when a sign needs to be interpreted by a third party, its meaning can become skewed and distorted. Throughout history, well-meaning individuals as well as those who had less than the best intentions manipulated the signs due to ignorance or self-advancement.

So, we learned quite some time ago to try to use very personal signs associated with a deceased loved one that only the individual who was to receive them would understand. We branched out with this method so that signs could also incorporate family and friends and even groups when that particular method was necessary.

So, it was decided that individual signs would be the best method to communicate from our side to yours. As generations went by, some of these signs became well known to the point where we are still able to use them today, as they have already been recognized as a method of communication.

Examples of this include the use of coins, feathers, and the animal kingdom. Since past generations have accepted the signs as coming from the afterlife, it has made it easier for current generations to recognize the signs and therefore be more willing to accept them.

Recognizing a sign is the first step in the communication process. If one recognizes that a sign may have come from a deceased loved one, it opens the lines of communication to the point where acceptance—that is, belief—can be achieved.

If we tried to use a new method of communication, it would have to be something that was extremely specific to both the individual who has passed and the one remaining on the Earth plane. Therefore, these other forms of communication are limited in their use. They may take the form of direct communication through voice. Some individuals are able to be used as a conduit between our world and yours. They are able to bring messages through using the actual voice of the deceased loved one. These messages can be shared with an individual or a group. These individuals are rare and are mostly used to demonstrate that this method still exists and can be used when necessary.

The use of signs as a communication method has resulted in the understanding that once an individual passes from the Earth plane existence back to their spiritual body, they can still communicate with those who have been left behind.

We will talk about many common signs we use to transfer this communication. Some of you may recognize some of these and have actually experienced these methods. For some others, these methods may be new or misunderstood. We hope to bring understanding about these methods in order to take the mystery away from how and why we use this method.

Signs are also a very easy form of communication. They are usually very short, precise, and specific. This makes them easier to understand and accept. At times a sign can be more complex and can involve other methods of communication. But these methods are not the norm and are used in specific situations. Everyday signs that occur to millions of people have been practiced, sharpened, and then perfected over time.

With each generation, we build on the communication that we have used in the past. We continually work on new methods of communication, and some of you alive today will see these before it is your time to pass over. These new methods will be used through the science of communication. By this, we mean communication methods that you use among yourselves on the Earth plane. We have been working on these for some time, and your technology has only now begun to enter the phase where we can implement these methods with a high level of success. The meaning of this method of communication will be evident when its use becomes open to the general population.

It is our intent to just provide background and understanding of these methods without going into the scientific makeup of the transfer of the messages.

Some of the stories you read in this book have been picked out by us in order for you to understand, in a practical way, how that particular method plays out. Also, it is important for those reading this book who have experienced signs themselves to see how others have experience similar signs.

The signs we use are of a universal nature. By this, we mean we can use some of these signs in all cultures and geographic locations on your plane of existence. Some are specifically adapted to a particular region or the beliefs of a particular culture. But the methods are the same, meaning we try to use objects and memories of each individual involved in the transfer of the communication.

Perhaps in one culture, a particular object or event might be used to send a sign that would not be used in a different culture. The method is the same, but the particular object or symbol would be different.

So, it is important to remember that not only are people in your particular culture or country receiving signs from deceased loved ones, but all humans throughout the Earth plane can and do receive signs from the afterlife. We use the word *afterlife* to signify a deceased loved one sending a sign back to a living loved one. Signs are still communicated from our side, which is the spiritual dimension of life, to your plane of existence by guides and teachers in order to help individuals and groups to grow and learn."

The Importance of Signs

Signs are very important to those who have lost children because they show that their children are still with them throughout their lives. Sometimes parents rely on signs in order to get through their day. This is not something we wish people to rely upon, but we realize it's a coping mechanism that some people use. In this book, we will explain other coping mechanisms that are available to the people who have lost children, but for now we will stay on the subject of signs.

By sending the signs, the children make clear that their awareness of the events that are going on in their parents' lives are current, and they can be a part of those events. They want to show their parents that even though they are not there physically, they are there mentally and spiritually and also have the ability to interact with them during their parents' daily lives.

By spiritually, we mean through a loving emotional bond. This is the essence of the connection. Many times the children can transfer their thoughts into the parents' awareness in order to create a closeness that the parents yearn for. The children are aware that the communications can sometimes can become blocked due to emotional stress around the passing. They are aware that certain times in the parents' lives are more intense than other times. Times such as birthdays, times of passing, family celebrations, and holidays are often times when emotional resistance to communication can be high.

But the children are aware of this and will work to give signs that the parents are able to witness and understand. They realize the emotional distress the parents are going through at these times and realize that they will have to create a perfect circumstance in order for their communications to be understood. An example of this is when a parent may be overwhelmed to the point of not being able to function in their daily activities. The child may step closer to the parent and comfort them on an emotional level, even though a classic sign is not necessarily witnessed. By this, we mean that the child's energy will try to coexist with the parents' energy fields in order to relieve some of the stress. Sometimes parents will feel a change of energy around them during certain periods of distress. This may be their child's energy or at times other loved ones coming closer within their energy field in order to relieve them of some of the burden they are experiencing at that time.

At other times, the children will send signs as a way to interact with a parent on a joyful level and bring happiness, laughter, and relief to the parent. So, these particular signs are not just a form of communication to let the parent know that they are still in existence; the signs are also a form of communication to evoke a physical response from the parent. An example is something that makes the parent smile or laugh. This is a physical response to a piece of communication. Communication can also be a simple hello to show that the child is still actively around the parent. Other forms of communication may evoke a physical change in the parents' energy. As discussed before, the purpose may be to increase the parents' energy to bring healing to them or to change the parents' energy and bring warmth and comfort.

So, there are different ways of communicating from our side to yours using various methods, including animals, smells, sounds, music, and so on. The children like to use many of these common symbols because their parents are already aware of their ability to be used.

[I'm now hearing a young child yell out, "We don't have to recreate the wheel."]

A little boy says this
"It makes it easier on us to talk to our parents this way than having them learn a whole new language. Mom can be really hard to deal with sometimes; she cries a lot and yells at dad. This is because my mom seems to be constantly fearful and anxious. So I try to calm my mom down and let her know I'm still around. She knows, but it's not the same as being there. But I still do it. I just wish she would understand that I'm right there talking to her as she's talking to herself."

Little girl, nine years old
"My mom tells me she loves me all the time. I hear it when she's happy and unhappy. When she's unhappy, I try to support her. When she's happy, I like to be around her because I get to laugh with her. So Mom, try to be happy so I can play with you more.

Teenage boy
Mom, I know it's hard. I can feel what you're feeling, and I need you to know that I'm fine. No really, I'm fine. I see you all the time. I can feel the loss that you have experienced. It's like a big hole in your energy field. I want to see you whole again so you can enjoy your life and I can enjoy it with you. But right now you're in a continuous healing state, and this takes a lot of energy,

Mom—a lot of energy from you and a lot of energy from me. I've seen other mothers who have healed up this hole that leaves a huge scar. It can be like a quarter of the size of your body.

The stitching that's used to close this hole is made with angelic thread. It is healed through your energy fields. It's made up of love, understanding, acceptance, and compassion. The main ingredient is compassion—compassion for others and, most importantly, compassion for yourself. This is the energetic suture that is used to close the energy hole that people experience with the loss of a child.

Some parents refuse to use this thread and wish for the hole to remain open and exposed. In these instances, healing can't occur, for the person's energy is constantly drained and the unit as a whole cannot function at a normal level. There are various reasons people do not accept the healing. One of these is self-hate; they feel as though they must punish themselves for the passing of the child.

On the subconscious level, they feel that this is their sentence that they deserve for the loss of a child. Over time they will begin to create the thread of healing, but for many it becomes an unfinished business and lies in pieces rather than being utilized for the healing process.

By reaching out to others and helping them, a parent can begin to manufacture the sutures of healing. With the realization that life continues both here and on the other side, the parent can realize that they are still a part of the growing process for both the child and themselves.

Once the parent realizes that they are still involved in the child's life, this awareness can close huge gaps in the hole that was created by the passing, for the parent realizes that they are still on some level responsible in helping the child continue to learn and grow. The child's passing does not relieve the parent of the responsibility of helping them. Children who have passed realize this and, depending on their level of development, they are able to help their parents move forward on their path.

Parents who doubt the process rely on different forms of self-help. Sometimes they put their power and trust in an individual higher being. Sometimes they try to disable their awareness and feelings surrounding the matter with the use of alcohol and drugs. Other times, they will take on self-destructive behavior to once again torment themselves.

Is It Authentic?

A real sign will cause a real emotional response—a WOW moment, the kind that gives you goosebumps. It could be a vivid dream that lasts many years—one that you still remember the details of as if it were last night.

You're thinking of your deceased loved one, and then all of a sudden, bang, there's a sign. Once they come through, they might repeat contact at the same time and place, and use the same sign. Examples of this are finding coins, repeated smells associated with your loved one, or perhaps sequential numbers showing up at a particular time every night or early in the morning.

Oftentimes, we doubt whether we have actually received a sign, even though we might be open to the possibility and truly believe we can receive a sign. This will often reduce the quality of that sign when you accept it. The strong, loving connection is weakened by your doubt.

Many times, signs will be blatantly obvious to us and others around us. We might think they would not send such an obvious sign, when in reality signs can be huge or as small as a whisper. So, if you truly believe that contact has been made, you can be reassured that it is an authentic sign.

When you believe, a loving connection develops between our side and their side, even if the sign you have recognized was not originally authentic. Just by truly believing a loving connection can be made, it will cause a sign to be instigated and created by ourselves.

If a sign is received around a particular special event such as a wedding or the birth of a child, there is a higher probability that the sign is authentic. Our deceased loved ones love to show that they are still in our lives and will therefore attempt to send signs around times of family gatherings or moments of remembrance. Holidays, birthdays, and specific places can all add weight to judging whether a sign is authentic.

[From Joe's book I Got Your Message]

Methods

⊹⊱⊰⊹

"Many times people have a close relationship with the natural surroundings of the physical plane. Within these boundaries are methods of contact that can be arranged to show a sign. We have the ability to intercede in the actions of the animal world as well as with plants and the weather. If someone would recognize a sign more easily due to the action of an animal or a significant flower or breeze, then this would be implemented in the type of contact. We are not limited as to the methods of contact, and we have vast interacting abilities within the physical plane."

One of the methods used by those who have passed is sound, such as music or a distinct noise the love one would connect to the person who has passed. Oftentimes a particular song will be played, as it brings up the emotional connection between the loved one who has passed and those who are left behind. It's their intention to use this method because music has a strong emotional connection on both our side and their side, and it can relate to past shared experiences. Music is deeply embedded in our sense of remembrance. Music can be used for group signs, too, as other family members may be aware of the connection at the same time. A natural sound such as waves crashing or raindrops may be used to quiet your mind so your loved one's connection can slip into your consciousness.

Another sign that they like to use is a scent or smell. This is one of the easiest and has a wide range of opportunities that can be tapped into, such as the smell of a cigar, perfume, or even a young girl's freshly shampooed hair. A smell may have different meanings to different people, but the one it is focused on will have the memory of a shared experience associated with it. Thus it can be used as we go about our everyday lives, even if we are distracted at a particular moment. It can cause us to stop what we are doing to analyze what is happening, and the connection has then been made.

Electricity is another easy form for people who have passed to manipulate in order to get our attention. A flickering light or perhaps an appliance that suddenly comes on is a quick, direct sign that can be sent by them to make us aware of their presence. It can take place through visual or audible means. By manipulating the energy flow around an object, they are able to change the tone, volume, and level of brightness. Kids like this form, as it can startle some people, and the kids get a giggle from doing it. I remember, as a child, going to bed with the TV on and the volume very low. I think it was a form of background noise to help me fall asleep. Almost every night, I would awaken a few hours later with the sound cranked up high. I'd usually say to myself, 'Can you guys not put it so high? You keep waking me up.' It was probably what they wanted to do in the first place.

Objects have been used throughout history to bring awareness of the presence of those who have passed. This can include personal items, coins, feathers, and any object that would bring your awareness to the possibility of your loved one being around you. They can pick out an everyday object in your home and bring your attention to it through movement. This can be done at certain times, perhaps around a holiday or a particular date of importance. A wedding picture frame could fall over on an anniversary, a school class photo may come into you awareness on a child's birthday, or coins may show up repeatedly in unexpected places. These signs can be subtle or obvious.

The easiest form of connecting to our side is through the use of dreams. When we sleep, many of our distractions are taken away, and we are in a better state to be able to accept contact from their side. Sometimes this cannot occur due to various sleep disruptions. However, it is one of the most commonly used forms of contact, as it allows them to appear and pass the message with the least amount of disruption. Some messages are a little more complex and need to be shared in the dream state as opposed to the other methods mentioned. Dreams are also used to connect with a friend or colleague when other attempts to make contact have not been successful. It is their intention for the friend to pass along the information that was shared with them, and thus a connection is made.

Daydreaming is a great way for a loved one to gain access to your consciousness, too, as it's a form of meditation. Your busy mind is slowed down, and a loved one can use this time to make contact. So, to all the people who say they have trouble meditating, practice daydreaming.

Often people will interpret numbers as a sign that a loved one is near. At times particular numbers will repeat in order for us to distinguish that a pattern has been established. Numbers related to anniversaries, birthdays, and special occasions will also appear as signs because loved ones know you will associate those things with them. Our modern lives are surrounded by numbers; dates, times, and age are just a few examples of how we live our lives in accordance with numbers. People will remember certain numbers associated with a passed loved one for the rest of their lives. So, it is easy to gain our attention by using a particular set of numbers, knowing we will make the connection to our deceased loved one, even if it is a common number used for another occasion.

At times they will also use their voice, with particular inflections so as to identify themselves. Everyone seems to have a particular way they speak, and they will use this individuality in order to grab our attention. This method is not used as often as some of the other signs mentioned, as it can at times be startling and cause anxiety. But a certain phrase once used by a loved one can be projected from another individual to gain your attention. It's not that they are using the other person's voice but rather putting that particular phrase into their consciousness to be spoken. The individual saying it might never had used that phrase before and may find it curious as to why they did just then. Hearing a distinct laughter similar to that of a deceased loved one is another common way of grabbing our attention. It's spirit's way of reaching out and getting our attention even if we're among many other people.

Special occasions such as anniversaries, birthdays, and holidays are always times when the energy is high and a loved one's wish is to contact us. If asked for a sign, some like to make their presence known and want you to know they are still around you and celebrating a particular occasion. If they feel that a sign at this time may bring unease or anxiety, they will enjoy your company but will not make themselves known. They do not want to bring stress or discomfort to any of us. But know that they are still there with us and continue to enjoy celebrating our lives.

So, the signs will be customized for each of us, depending on our shared memories and experiences with the loved one who has passed. At other times, they can actually send a sign to a group of people. This can happen at family gatherings, social affairs, and even community events. This happens when more than one person would be able to recognize the sign, and it magnifies the strength of the sign, as people will discuss how they noticed it and how it was a shared sign. When people discuss the signs they have received from deceased loved ones, it brings empowerment not only to themselves but also to those who may have received a sign but have not made their observations public.

Many of these types of signs have been used throughout history and are recognized as being associated with contact with a deceased loved one. Coins and feathers are commonly recognized objects that can be used and recognized by many, even in different cultures and societies.

Some methods have been more heavily relied upon during other time periods. For instance, coins were used at one time as a sign but had to be discontinued, as their meaning became corrupted and people believed they contained pieces of magic.

However, in modern times, the use of coins has returned as a favorite method of connecting and is often shown in cultural themes.

With the use of modern technology such as cell phones and Wi-Fi, the methods that can now be incorporated have greatly expanded. Phones can ring, messages can be left, and all sorts of manipulation is possible.

So, the manifestation of signs will continue to grow and adapt, depending on the times we live in. By sharing the signs with each other, we can make more people aware of how common they actually are. Oftentimes people believe they have received a sign but are afraid to admit it because they think they may be ridiculed. The more of us who share a sign story, the more power these people will have to open up and relay their experiences. And in doing so, they can begin to heal and accept the peace that can come about by receiving a sign.

[*Channeled from my guides*]

"The reason that these specific methods of contact were chosen was to give you an idea of the variety of ways we can go about trying to communicate with you. We have noticed that the majority of people possess the ability to recognize signs once they have understood these explanations. It is not our intention to try to make the connections more difficult than they need to be, so we like to use familiar things that you interact with in your daily lives."

One of the most important things I've learned about signs is that you don't have to receive one to understand their meaning. If others are sharing their sign stories with you, it must be noted that our love ones also continue to exist and continue to be part of our daily lives.

There are many reasons that we as individuals do not receive a particular sign. Some of these reasons may be due to deep grief, stress, or even because of limitations put on us for cultural and religious reasons. But by hearing the stories of others who have been in contact with their deceased loved ones, we can understand that it truly does happen. And once we understand this, we know that all of our loved ones are also by our side and do not cease to exist.

Children's Insights

Today we would like to give the kids the opportunity to tell you, in their own words, how they interact so you can listen to each of their stories. This way, you can understand their perspective as told from a first-person point of view.

Amy

Joe, this is Amy. She died when she was thirteen. Her dad and mom are not living together anymore. They divorced since her passing. They both need to hear from her at certain particular times. She tries to connect with them on holidays and special occasions like birthdays, both his and hers. At times she finds it difficult because they're at different levels of understanding with regard to the process of crossing over. So she can talk to her dad in a different way than her mother. Dad wants to analyze whether it's possible to still talk with her.

"Mom understands that the feelings she gets are coming from me, but she still has doubts. Oftentimes I try to connect them together so they can see that we're *all* still connected. Just because they don't live with each other doesn't mean we aren't all still connected. To do this, I sometimes will urge them to communicate with each other about me. Yeah, I can use my passing as leverage, ha ha, to get them to talk. I know it sounds crazy, and it is, ha ha.

Dad will listen to me sometimes when he is listening to music. I'll make sure his favorite songs are being played, and then I can slip into his consciousness, as it's easier that way to get through. I don't have to tap him on the shoulder or yell in his ear either, ha ha. I can give him a simple nudge to let him know I'm around. When he feels calm and light, that's when I like to be around and let him know I'm there. It's easier that way. Other times when there is too much commotion, it's impossible to get through; it's like a thick wall. The darker emotions are the most difficult. When they're feeling stressed or hateful about something, even just being stuck in traffic, it can block us from coming through. So, we have to choose our places very carefully; otherwise, it takes up too much energy to try to get through.

With Mom, it's a little bit easier, as she is more open to the possibility that I'm around. She sometimes asks me to send a sign, which is great because that makes it a lot easier. When she asks, I just have to "dial one up" and there it is. She will sometimes miss some of the signs, but that's okay, as I can to send another one. She doesn't want to believe I'm gone, so she stays open to receiving anything I send her way. It's not just that she misses me; it's that she feels as if I'm not with her. But in reality, I am with her. I can be right next to her while she's cooking if she wants. Other times, I can be somewhere else and still hear her and feel her. So don't misunderstand that because we are not there physically, we're not there emotionally or mentally. We can hear you guys and we can feel you. Let yourselves do the same for us. It's okay to cry about us, but don't think we're not here, because we are."

Trevor

Joe, this is Trevor. Trevor passed when he was seventeen or eighteen, near his birthday.

"It was kind of a celebration of my birthday. I just want to say how I love how all this works. When I got here, I was shown how to send signals to my mom and dad and that I could do it at certain times in their lives. Some days are easier than others, depending on their moods. I'll try at night with my mom because she's more able to accept them at that time. With my dad, it's easier to send them at work because he notices things that don't fit in while he's in those surroundings, so the signs stand out.

Sometimes Mom will reach out to me and asked for a sign letting her know I'm around by giving her different signs. Sometimes I talk to her and she can hear me. Other times if she's watching TV, I'll have my name on a commercial or show. She thinks I'm doing that on purpose and I am, ha ha. Mom sometimes knows when I'm around and senses it, and at other times she can't pick it up. If she's busy in the middle of something, I can slip by and say hi, and she'll pick it up. But other times if she's with neighbors or friends, I won't try because most of the time she won't notice. She knows I'm around, but I don't want to interrupt her while she's having fun. And it really helps if they're having fun because the energy around them becomes finer, so it's easier for us to send a sign. When they're not having fun, their energy is denser.

It's like trying to skip a rock on the water and using a big hunk of coal as opposed to a skimmer rock. If the water is calm and smooth, we can skip right on by and leave our mark. But if the water is rough, the rocks will just crash, and they won't be able to know we said hi."

Mary

Now we have Mary. Mary is fourteen and is very demonstrative. [Being shown acting for emphasis]

"I love it when I get to send a sign; it's so cool. I get to pick the time and how it's going to be done. I have so much fun deciding how I want to make my presence known. Sometimes I can be playful and move things around; other times I can be more direct and just yell out her name. Once when Dad was trying to lift up the couch to find something, I said that he'd hurt his back. I put this in his mind, and he just dropped the couch, knowing that this was going to happen. The dog ran out of the room, and I started to giggle. Dad didn't realize it was me, but if I hadn't said something, he would have hurt his back. He has back problems, and I just wanted to make sure he wasn't going to be in pain for the rest of the week. But other times I can sing and they will hear me. They know this because I used to sing around the house when I was happy. So they will hear the humming sound of my voice in their head and think that's what I used to do. What I'm actually doing is singing to them. Other times I'll play with the dog. I like to play with his ears. Sometimes he likes it, but sometimes he runs away. Ha ha.

Dad doesn't understand why I had to leave and asked that question over and over. He sometimes just wants a simple answer. There are no simple answers; it's confusing and complex at times, but just knowing that we're still around is the most important thing.

There are lots of kids over here who, like me, love giving signs. You just have to be open to them and realize it's possible. Thank you.

Tom

"I'm Tom. My brother was Timmy. I passed first, before my brother. He was left behind, and I tried to contact him right away after I left. He didn't understand the signs, even though we had similar interests, and I tried to use those as signs.

Timmy didn't want to believe I was gone and started to have doubts about his own life. This is one of the reasons he crossed over after I did. He felt alone and felt that he couldn't handle what was happening in his own life, so he decided to end it. He sometimes says hi to Dad now but mostly stays with his newfound friends on this side. He's learning about the cause of his transition and why he did it at that particular time. He wants everyone to know that he felt guilty at the time of his crossing and soon realized it's not something he could have foreseen. This helped with his transition a lot. He thinks it's okay to send signs, but he doesn't want to upset anyone he left behind. So he only sends them once in a great while. I try to send signs pretty often, but sometimes I get distracted and forget to tap back in. I have many interactions with your side. Sometimes I'm more focused on helping people heal than on looking for a particular person and offering them a sign. I work with other children who passed suddenly, so my goal is to integrate with them as soon as possible so they can transition as easily as possible. Once they get to our side, we can help them much more efficiently than when they were on your side. I left when I was twenty-six, but I can relate to children who are younger than me because I've been through this situation many times and understand where they were coming from. Many times it's just an accident, while at other times there was much suffering before they left. And the hole that they created when they left needs to be addressed as well.

Many who are left behind have lots of questions and few answers, and that's why I asked to be able to give this information to you—so you could let others know that we are aware of the difficulties of trying to understand the whole process of when a child dies. It's not just the loss of a loved one in the family circle, but also how it affects those left behind in every aspect of their lives. So, someone who did not have children can and does get affected when one of their friends, colleagues, or loved ones loses their child. Many times people don't realize this.

So by talking about it and bringing it to light, we can help those who at times suffer in silence, not wanting to interfere with the grief process of those directly involved. Many times those involved will not understand the grieving process of those who were not connected to the child who has passed, so we must remain diligent in helping these people because they suffer as well.

It's important to realize that with any passing, people will feel a loss of hope. We wish for you to understand that this is not hope that is lost—it's only the physical body.

We take the position of trying to help you in your physical body go through this natural phase of crossing over. We become teachers, counselors, and social workers who try to hold together your experience on the life plane. You usually don't see it that way while living there but only gain this knowledge after crossing over. The knowledge in actuality is the new perspective—a wider perspective with more depth.

So it's a constant interaction between your side and our side, with signs, requests, and observations coming and going. It's just a different form of connection. And as we try to explain these different forms of communications, all we ask is that you consider the larger picture—the bigger perspective of life in general.

No one is ever lost—they just moved to a different city."

Sign Stories

Dreams

He's always leaving signs. When the pandemic first started, I was at my parents' home in Florida on vacation. I didn't know what to do—I had my vacation booked for a week, and I didn't know whether I should stay put or fly home. I was scared and panicked to the point that I was making myself sick every day. I was overthinking, had a lot of fear, and was so anxiety ridden that I was giving myself asthma attacks.

I felt alone, but then I had a dream that was so real. I really thought I could have died. I was floating on clouds with Nicholas. We were flying, talking, and laughing—everything was so beautiful. He told me not to be scared, not to listen to everything I was hearing, and to follow my own intuition. He said the answers were there and to start using my gifts. "Some learn them; some are born with them," he said.

He started to let my arm go as if he was reaching away from me, and I slowly started being out of reach, but I continued to try to get his hand back. He then looked at me and asked, "What is your choice—to stay with me or stay with Josh and Gavyn?" It was the hardest decision, but I told him I had to stay here. He then started to float again and said, "That was the choice you were supposed to make. The ultimate sacrifice. Now, do not be afraid anymore; now live, and shortly after Easter things will start looking up." It's crazy—I don't know what happen and whether I died or whether it was a dream. Whatever it was, I was no longer afraid.

I starting to go with my intuition and found that whatever happen to me that night in Florida was more real than I can explain, and what Nick was telling me was that I needed to learn to use my intuition. And by learning, my fear level continued to decline. But whatever is going on with me, those dreams feel so real. I became unafraid and instead became curious about what's really happening in the world around us.

In memory of Nicholas Silva Thomas

Author

Melissa knew in her soul that she needed to stay—that there was other work to be done before she left the Earth plane. Nicholas, now knowing his mother's soul plan to a certain degree, put the question to her. By asking her, it reinforced Melissa's connection to her goals, even if she was not conscious of them. What great insight from a son to his mom about the realization that staying on the Earth plane was the true answer. Tremendous growth was available to her through "the ultimate sacrifice." I also think it's great wisdom to replace fear with curiosity, as Melissa mentioned.

The Butterflies

The butterflies started to follow me the first summer after my son died in April. The second time I noticed it while I was walking, I said, "If that is you, Doug, fly close to me." I stood still, and it came within inches of me and flew off. My hubby and I went to the beach in September. The beach was Doug's favorite vacation place. We also spread some ashes at the beach. We were playing horseshoes when about six beautiful butterflies flew right between us. We both knew it was a sign. Then last September something similar happened. We were walking and a butterfly started to follow us. Then when we sat on the beach, and it came and rested on the sand right next to us. As soon as spring hits, the butterflies find me again. I always see them on books and cloths and all over.

In memory of Doug Paul from Mom

Author

When Doug first used this sign, it was recognized immediately by his mom, so he repeated it. This is very common, so be aware if it happens to you. Also, by having butterflies show up at his favorite location (the beach), it is easier to make a connection to him and let his parents know that when they go on vacations, he'll be going, too!

Sounds & Cardinals

A few days after my son's funeral when his dad went out for the first time, I woke up from being sound asleep to the stereo blasting.

I ran downstairs and clicked it off. I know that was Doug. It hasn't happened since. My hubby thought it was a sign. I am sure it was. Doug never used the stereo, and my hubby had not touched it for a while. But, Doug knew I used it a lot. I have recorded my own songs with it. Also regarding songs, certain groups that he loved will play out of nowhere, such as when I'm at work—groups that don't fit the station I'm listening to.

The guys who were my son's friends brought over a tree to plant in my backyard in remembrance of him. About a month later, I was getting in my car in the driveway, and I was thinking about Doug and then heard a bird rustling. I looked over, and it was a red cardinal jumping around in a tree. I had never even seen one before. It comes all the time now. Even on vacation last week, a cardinal came in all three spots where we stayed. I took some pics. My son loved to go on vacation with us, and we did visit a place where he had been with us. But I also saw cardinals in two places he had never been with us. I know he is always with me, so I wasn't surprised to see the cardinal. It was wonderful.

In memory of Doug Paul from Mom

Author

Sounds are an easily recognized sign to send, as sound is hardwired into our survival mode. We can pick it up while in the middle of other activities. Cardinals are another method of contact that has been embedded in our culture. By using this sign, the chances of recognition will be higher than with some other methods.

Pennies & Lights

Pennies show up just when it's important. When I found a penny the first time, it was a very sad time about one month after my son's death. I was at work waitressing and found it while cleaning up at the end of the night, bright and shining under a table. It was 2015—the year he died. It made me feel really good, so I'm very sure it was him.

The lights flicker. The fire alarm will start , but the battery is fine, and then it won't do it for a long time. I could be sitting here watching TV after my hubby goes to sleep, and it will go off behind me. I just say, "HI, Dougy."

My dog stares right past me at least once a day. I'll say, "Is Dougy here?" and my dog will just turn and stare. I get so many signs, I can't remember them all.

In memory of Doug Paul from Mom

Author

Coins in general, and pennies in particular, are a very common sign, as they have been use for hundreds of years. They're one of the methods that have become part of our culture, so their recognition doesn't have to be questioned as deeply as some other methods.

Kids are very good at manipulating electricity. That's because it creates such a dramatic effect, and the kids love seeing their loved ones' reactions. They really get a kick out of it.

The Kingfisher

We saw unusual birds when we went for a walk every day. My son was an avid bird photographer, and his knowledge of birds and other animals was impeccable. We had thick foliage outside my room's balcony, where he used to spend hours trying to capture beautiful birds with his camera. We don't live in a coastal region, and kingfishers are unheard of here. One day, my husband and I noticed a beautiful blue kingfisher sitting in the trees. Soon a residential scheme was planned, and all the foliage was removed. We lost hope of seeing the bird again. We put out a bowl of water and some grains for the birds who had lost homes. And a month ago, the kingfisher returned to drink from the bowl. I was ecstatic. A week later, my husband spotted it again. And yesterday we both saw it perched on a small branch. It stayed there long enough for both of us to absorb the sight. But my logical brain was skeptical. Was it really my son sending it? That afternoon, as I was going through his Instagram account (which I have done almost on daily basis since he passed), I noticed for the first time a picture of this kingfisher, which he had posted on June 6, 2015!!!! I didn't need further validation.

Joe, as I write this, it has been therapy for me, too, as my faith in my son's presence has been reinforced. Suzanne Giesemann is a medium to whom I wrote in October and was not expecting to hear from, as she has a waiting period of months and often years for a reading. But in November I had a mailing from her telling of an opening for December 8! My son came through her very poignantly and said that he was instrumental in getting me to her!!

In memory of my son, Smayan

Author

Since her son was an avid bird photographer, it is not surprising to see he used a bird to gain her attention. They do try to use the easiest method for us to recognize their signs, as our lives can be so busy that we might otherwise miss their attempts to connect.

License Plate & Image

I was driving through Georgia, looking at the clouds, and asking for a sign from my daughter Karla. Nothing—then I looked down, and the car in front of me had a license plate that said "pinky." That's my daughter's nickname!

Another time we were driving down the highway, and I asked for a sign from Karla. I happened to look over at a car passing us, and the woman turned her head and smiled. It was Karla! I screamed and said, "It's Karla—catch up with that car." Well, when we caught up and looked again, it was an older woman, nothing like my young daughter. But I knew it was her sending me her smiling face as a very special sign. It was incredible.

In memory of Karla

Author

How many times do we try to pick the time and place for a sign? Here is a good example of trying to force a sign and then when she let go, bam, there it was.

Although rarer than some other methods of sending a sign, it is not totally unheard of to see a loved one's face on another individual's body. When it does happen, it's usually a quick sighting but is long enough to express a reaction to others in the area. It's happen to me, and it was witnessed by another person sitting in my car. Thanks, James—we saw you.

―――

Mom Needs a New Phone

My son, Smayan, was a happy, healthy, and lively fifteen-year-old teenager. On June 6, 2017, he developed a viral fever, and after almost three weeks passed away in the hospital due to respiratory and multi-organ failure. We lost the joy of our lives. He had a twin sister, and our square became a triangle.

I am a technologically backward person, and he was a gadget freak. He always wanted me and his dad to use the best devices and have the best things. I was using the same cell phone for three years, and he desperately wanted me to buy a new one. Before he had the fever, he was pestering me to replace my old phone, but I kept avoiding it. I felt that as long as it was working, I didn't need to spend the money. Then, as he had the fever and was sick at home, he kept on searching for a new phone for me on various online sites.

He had to be admitted to the hospital a few days after, and I had promised him that as soon as we got home, he could find a new phone for me and I would order it online. But he passed away on the June 27.

I soon realized that my phone was misbehaving. The screen was becoming unresponsive to my touch, and it was acting weird. This went on for two days. Then on the day we were to immerse his ashes, the phone stopped responding completely. I had to replace it immediately. My husband and I immediately knew that Smayan got his desire fulfilled.

In memory of my son, Smayan

Author

A conversation about a specific topic can be a great sign to send through after a passing. Here we see Smayan using this method, as well his own desire, to have his mom's phone replaced.

Section VII

Healing

"The energy that nature gives off has a healing effect on the human body—physically, emotionally, and even spiritually."

J.M. Higgins

Love Is Infinite

This is something that comes to mind often when someone loses a child. When we see someone questioning themselves with respect to losing the love, the person asking the question is relating the concept of love with that particular individual. When this happens, the complexities of the loving bond become more finite, which will cause the recipient to believe that loving bond has separated or is broken because of the child's passing.

We would like to share the concept that love is infinite. It is not something that can be broken, lost, or dissolved. Oftentimes we see people who want to understand love as a direct association with an individual, place, or event. When they do this, they place time constraints around the concept of love.

That is why you hear expressions such as "lost love," "I love the good old days," and "Will I ever find love again?" In actuality, love is constant. But how the individual wants to classify it can get them in trouble. And when we say "trouble," we mean that by classifying it, you are putting restraints on it and limiting its potential.

So, when an individual passes—in this case, a child—that loving bond that was created at birth or through association with that child is believed to be broken. It is this belief that causes much of the grief and continuation of suffering for those left behind.

You see, people use their own understanding of love to create how they will react in situations in which this love may change form or appearance. So, the individual has a preconceived concept about how love plays out and is able to actualize this process and then react to their perception.

What we are trying to say is that you need to change your perception of how love—in this case, the loving bond with the child—actually works.

When a child passes over, no matter the circumstances, the love that they have created does not diminish or change. People have a tendency to put a beginning and an ending on many aspects of their lives. In the case of a passing, this is not accurate.

When a child passes, the energy surrounding the passing can be of a higher, more acute sense than when someone passes who has lived many decades on the Earth plane. But the process is very similar. That loving bond is consistent over the bridge of life on your plane and the spiritual plane of the child. The love continues to flow back and forth. The child can feel the love of those left behind, and those who are still here on the Earth plane can continue to feel the love of the child.

What must be separated is the fact that missing the individual is separate from the love of that individual. It is difficult to be used to seeing someone, especially someone you care for very much, and then they are no longer there. The physical connections and the associations are all intermingled with another individual. When death occurs, that separation is realized as a final point. It is to a certain extent true, especially concerning the interaction of the physical bodies.

The events associated with that person continue on in your

memories. Your interaction with the individual will continue, even though the physical body is not present. This is very important to understand. You can still interact with your child, even though the physical presence is not felt.

Some learn to feel the presence of the child or are open enough to believe that this can occur. The child will still be involved in your life for long as you walk the Earth plane. They can intercede, can be involved, and can give you insight into new aspects of your life. The communication and interaction with you are just different from how they were while here on the Earth plane.

Remember, the love is constant. Just because you cannot see the individual does not mean the love has stopped. The child can support you in your time of need if you're willing to open your heart and accept the fact that they are still with you and will be with you throughout your time. They can hear and feel your sorrow, and they can feel your happiness and joy. It is important to remember that what you bring into yourself in association with them is as though they were sitting right next you and going through the process themselves.

If you're sad because you miss their presence, they will understand this because they have the perspective of seeing how the lack of physical interaction affects individuals on the Earth plane. However, when they see a parent or loved one continue to struggle from having lost them, they have a difficult time continuing on the path they need to take. By this, we mean that the work they need to continue can be stunted by the energy you have attached to that loving bond. In other words, they can feel your unhappiness and despair.

In actuality, your unhappiness and despair travel through that loving energy bond and resonate within their essence, causing them discomfort. This is not the same as going through the grief process that is associated with the passing of a loved one from the Earth plane back to the spiritual realm. The normal stages of grief are well understood on the other side, and they try to bring us some relief as we move through them.

But the child does not want to see an individual's life disrupted to the point where they cannot move forward on their path of learning and achieve some of the goals they have set out to achieve when they came to the Earth plane. That child, who is a whole spiritual being on the other side, will feel burdened that their interaction with that parent, sibling, or other individual has caused the stunting of development for those left behind.

The parent still has the responsibility to the child, even after the transition. There is still an active connection. You have a responsibility to yourself and them to continue on your life path and try to create joy and peace for yourself, others, and your deceased child.

The love that has been perceived to have been lost is never lost. This is the first step in understanding that the loving bond will continue throughout your life. Do not put a start/stop description to your relationship with the child.

The relationship is a continuation, just in a different form. Your interaction with them will continue—it is just something new that you must learn and understand. There can be great love and peace once this understanding is achieved. There is a special connection that is extremely intimate between you and the child who has passed.

So, begin to look at the situation not as a love lost but rather as a new love found. When this happens, joy and happiness will return to a special level that will increase over time as you realize that this wonderful, beautiful, loving energy that was a part of you still lives and will grow with you as you experience new adventures in your lifetime.

There is no lost love—just a different appearance.

Healing Through Health

We want to outline a few healing practices that people can utilize to reduce the discomfort they are experiencing with the loss of a child.

Some of these exercises and examples will work for some but not others. Some individuals have a high degree of ability to accept and initiate change in their lives, while others have a more pronounced way of thinking of how things ought to be. There is no correct or incorrect way; whichever approach works for an individual is what is most important.

As we have discussed previously, everyone grieves in a different way and through a different process. Therefore, healing will come in different ways and through different processes. Some approaches may seem redundant, while others might seem to be too "out of the box" for some people to even try. It is our intention to give you these options and leave the implementation of them up to you.

So, first we would like to focus on the **physical body**.

It is important to keep one's physical body in the best possible condition throughout the grieving process. Certain chemical reactions can increase the depth of grief by altering different hormones and reactions throughout the body. Other times, nutritional substances can cover up deep-seated feelings that need to be addressed.

In order to achieve maximum ability in creating one's life, keeping the human body in its best condition always gives the individual more opportunities to learn during life. We realize that learning is often accomplished through disease and other maladies of the physical body, but we will not be talking about that right now.

We want you to bring attention to how you are feeling physically—not emotionally, not mentally, but your actual physical body. Do you have aches and pains? Do you stumble when you walk? Is your body reacting as it did earlier in your life?

When an individual begins to grieve, it can have massive effects on the physical structure of the human body. We see this with chronic illnesses, autoimmune diseases, and lapses in judgment.

In order to take a step forward and bring relief and healing to some of what you're going through, we ask that you focus on your physical body and attempt to make it as well prepared as you can. We realize that many of you have conditions that will not allow your body to function as you would like. But what we ask is that you do not add to the discomfort of your physical body during this time. By doing so, it will create more discomfort and more problems that don't need to be created.

Start by doing the simple things, such as getting enough rest, eating properly, and getting exercise. Of course, we realize that you're sleep patterns will be off, depending upon where you are in the grieving process. So when we say get enough rest, it does not necessarily mean sleeping at night. Rest can also take place in the form of relaxation—listening to your favorite music, perhaps painting, or working out in nature. Anything that relaxes you is a form of rest.

Exercise, as we all know, creates many different positive outcomes relative to the physical and mental well-being of the human body. It is of greater importance at this time to realize that the physical body needs activity and attention so it can take on the added burden of the grief process. It is not necessary to run a marathon in order to bring healing to oneself. It might mean going for a walk once a day, taking a bike ride, or doing some resistance training. Anything that causes your muscles to contract and relax will alter your breathing and help your physical body. A little bit can go a long way.

Nature is one of the healing forces that all of you share on the Earth plane. It can be used throughout your life in dealing with major as well as minor challenges. It can be used to enhance one's mental capacities as well as reduce overall stress in the human body.

Being a part of nature, whether outside or inside, will create an environment of healing. This healing can take place on a conscious or subconscious level. Some people find it relaxing to be around plants or anything that's living, while others find comfort in sunshine or perhaps a rainstorm.

Use all of these to help yourself connect with nature and continue to use these throughout your life. The more you participate in using nature and physical activity, the more your human body will react positively. It is one step in a greater plan to help you deal with life's uncertainties.

Remember also that what you put into your body, both physically and mentally, will affect your physical condition. If you listen to upsetting information or something that annoys you or brings you discomfort, that will upset your physical body, so we advised against it. If you are constantly eating foods that cause discomfort or create chemical imbalances that change your moods, this should also be avoided, for the chemical reactions that take place in the human body from outside influences may either heal or cause trouble in the physical structure.

It is important to remember to take care of your physical body, as it will then help take care of your emotional and mental faculties. They all work together, and when one is out of balance, it will cause the others to also be out of balance. Once you realize this, you can take steps to help yourself or others begin the path back to healing yourself.

It is also important to take time for yourself. Many times people are forced to grieve and also interact with others on a daily basis. We realize that this is not always avoidable. However, you can and should make time for yourself to bring ease and relaxation into your life. When some of you say, "I don't have time to be alone," we say you do—you just have to find it. It can be a few minutes here and a few minutes there, but let that be **your** few minutes. When you can catch your own thoughts, take a few deep breaths, or smile at memories you have shared with your loved one who has passed, this will help you. Little things like this add up and should be utilized for the rest of your life. Use these tips for yourself as well as for others whom you see suffering. Not everyone will be able to always do everything that is right for their physical body, but once you start being aware of how things are connected, you will realize that even the simplest steps can make a huge difference in how you feel.

We have talked about the physical body and how important it is to keep it in the best condition in order to enhance the healing process and how important it is to pay attention to this while in the grieving process.

Now we want talk about how important it is to also focus on your **emotional well-being**. By this, we mean the overall feeling you have on a day-to-day basis coming from within yourself. Your emotions will have many ups and downs throughout your life, depending on certain situations. They are there to guide you during different environmental situations. Many times these emotions are created and utilized for your safety and to make you aware of certain opportunities that arise. The human body often needs additional information in order to survive, either for its own protection or in seeking out nutrients and other substances. Emotions play a role in both of these.

However, during the grief process, one's emotions can go in many different directions at the same time. The circumstances around the passing of a loved one will often create doubt about one's own place in life. Some people can rationalize certain situations more easily than others. All of them will go through different emotions, depending on their individual makeup. Some people feel and are more sensitive to certain stimuli, while others are more analytical in dealing with life's challenges.

It is important to try to keep one's emotions in balance in order to proceed with the life activities that need to continue. Unbalanced emotions can be debilitating to many, and this is of great concern to others who are trying to support you at this particular time.

There are certain things you can do to help yourself and try to balance out the emotional roller coaster that you may be experiencing. As with the physical body, your emotional makeup can vary, depending upon your nutritional needs as well as how much rest you get. We talked about taking time for yourself; this is very important when it comes to your emotional makeup. Other times, it is important to be around people, as they will stimulate you in showing their support. The love and understanding that others will offer you can bring great emotional balance and healing. Try to engage with people who bring this about and try to avoid others who may do the opposite and cause you more distress.

Being around others can be both a healing balm and distressing.

We want you to focus on the healing aspect of being with others. Focus on the community that has come together to support you throughout your grieving, no matter how long it takes, for many of these people are also going through the grieving process in a different way but are still feeling your loss. They, too, can gain healing by being allowed to assist you. Helping you will aid in healing their emotional distress, as the act of giving is a prime healing opportunity that is available to all on the Earth plane.

Emotional distress over a long period of time can create disease and disrupt the human mechanism to the degree where it is unable to take advantage of life's opportunities. Overall it's a part of the human system that is necessary in order to survive, but it also must be dealt with and conditioned in order not to take down the whole system. Plenty of rest, eating well, and interactions with people who care about your situation are just a few of the ways that healing can take place. The passing of a child can be a very complex situation where outside resources and actions or inactions can create problems for the emotional system. We do not want to get too complicated with these explanations because we want you to focus more on some of the simple things you can do to bring yourself more peace.

It is important to remember that dealing with your emotions during the passing of a loved one should be like riding a wave. This is a natural phenomenon, and to be aware of it will decrease the chances of the highs and lows that can bring additional grief. Love has always had an intense healing effect on everyone. By giving and making yourself available to receive love, the emotional system can recalibrate, thus giving you a reprieve from the ups and downs of everyday life. That is why we often talk about how giving of oneself to others and helping them heal can bring great healing back to yourself.

Many times we see parents, loved ones, and friends create

memorials, charities, and organizations for children who have passed. They put their emotions and focus in giving to others by doing this. By reaching out in this way, they create a ripple of good deeds in memory of their loved one. They create an action from the love they shared with their child. As the love continues between the person and the child who passed, that love can continue in different forms to bring about healing and peace to many others. Some may bring awareness to certain activities that might help save another child's life and save the parents or loved ones grief. Others may support certain organizations that will bring peace and healing to not only children but to adults and even pets. This is love being shown in different modalities. It is giving, and it not only spreads healing and peace but also feeds each individual who is participating in such activities.

We do not want people to feel they are obligated to create certain organizations after the passing of a loved one. This responsibility can cause much distress and anxiety. Instead, you may participate in others' actions, which, in itself, will bring you peace and comfort. Whatever feels more comfortable to you is the right thing to do. We do not want to see you in more distress by thinking you have certain obligations you must perform. Sometimes just accepting help and love from others is all you need to do. It can be that simple—open your heart and allow love from others to come in and thus begin to heal you and bring peace into your life.

Sometimes the simple things are all that is needed in a complex situation. Many wish to analyze and dictate a certain course of action, depending on certain circumstances for certain people at certain times. But this is not always necessary. Trust your instincts, and trust that the love you shared with the child continues, even if their physical body is no longer on the Earth plane. Love never dies.

The children on the other side will also attempt to bring healing and peace to you. That is why trying to keep emotional balance will allow them to intercede and bring you some of the healing that is necessary for you to continue on your life's journey. If you are physically or emotionally unable to accept this love from the other side, it can prolong the grieving process.

Connecting with Our Side

The easiest way to communicate with us is by opening your heart and allowing us to come through that loving portal into your consciousness. What we mean by this is that you're allowing us to have permission to contact you. It opens the door for the beginning of the communication lessons and to engage with you and communicate with you at our discretion. If someone does not wish to communicate with our side, we have no authority to try to contact that person. It has been done, and at times it does happen, but this is not the normal, everyday routine, as you would put it. You have total control over how the communication will be viewed.

We have seen that one of the easiest ways to communicate with our side is through telepathy or a simple thought. That's all it takes—just a simple thought about one of your loved ones, and you have opened up the communication channel. On our side of existence, we can feel your emotions, your thoughts, your prayers. It is much easier for us to receive your sign than the opposite: you receiving a sign from us. At other times, it's just as easy to communicate with sounds, smells, and touch as well as other avenues.

So take time out of the day to sit, relax, and quiet your mind.

This will give us time to learn the patterns of your thoughts in order to find the best possible time to communicate with you.

Prayer, a basic form of connecting with our side, is the main means of communicating with us, and this can be done anytime, day or night, and from any place.

If you wish to connect with us, setting a specific time, day, or routine would work well. It's like going to a classroom at a certain time to learn a new lesson. We will be there for you if you decide to do some learning every day at a particular time or every other day or whatever your schedule allows. Remember, the more you do it, the better you become at it. For others, brief contact is all that is requested, and this is all that we can request to happen, as it may be enough for the individual to realize that their spiritual being is not limited to the physical world and that they are in tune to the whole, the divine, from which they have come.

Write down questions you may have and ask them before you go to bed. The dream state is good way for us to connected with you. Keep a journal by your bedside so that when you awake, you can write down any insights you might have received. Some of your questions may be answered during the day by just popping into your mind as you're driving or partaking in a repetitive activity. Many people can receive information and communications from their guides and loved ones while doing one of their favorite activities, such as gardening, jogging, painting, or working on a puzzle. Anything that puts you in "the zone," as they say, works best. This is the time when you forget everything except the one thing you're doing. You have blocked out your everyday thoughts and responsibilities. It's a form of meditation. You're actively doing one thing but have also allowed your consciousness to wander. This is an active form of daydreaming. It's a wonderful state to be open to receiving communications from our side.

For more traditional methods, there are several types of meditations and yoga practices. Learning the practice of meditation and relaxation is very beneficial to the human body as well as the spirit. We say the spirit because when the human body is relaxed and not concerned with outside stimuli, it is focusing on learning, and the spirit grows through learning and lessons that have been created for it to discover and explore.

Now it's just a matter of practice, perseverance, and willingness to gain a level of communication you feel comfortable with in order to communicate with our side. Everyone has the ability to communicate with us. And when I say "us," I mean your guides, your loved ones, and the higher realms of consciousness.

Your ability to communicate is unlimited. However, the obstacles you can put in the way are also unlimited. It is you who must decide if you wish to open that door and learn to access the bridge that has always been there.

Pets & Healing

Pets have always had an unusual connection with humans in general as well as particular individuals. Sometimes the connections people have with their pets are as strong if not stronger than the connections they have with other human beings. This is not to say that pets are a replacement for human connection, but they may be the only source of love that is available at a particular time.

When we say pets, this is a general term that we will be using for relationships between human beings and the animal kingdom. Our focus today will be on domesticated animals, as you call them—the ones living within a person's home or environment.

The connections that people have with their pets are very similar to the interactions they have with their fellow human beings. They are conscious of their pet's movements, their needs, and their surroundings. The relationship they share with the pet can range from simple feeding and taking care of the pet's physical aspects to interacting and sharing a loving bond with the pet.

There is an energetic connection in this type of relationship that can bring out some of the hidden tools that a human has at birth, for example, intuition and the ability to sense when others are in need

This relationship promotes oversight, concern, and the ability to think about someone other than oneself.

All forms of love are active in a human-pet relationship. They include compassion, insight, and the ability to want the other to be happy and at peace.

The perspective of the pet is that they have accepted their human partner as one who will care for them and bring them joy at needed times. In return, the pet will use its insights and instincts to know when the human needs interaction and assistance. So there's a give-and-take to this type of partnership on both sides.

At certain times in one's life span, pets can bring great joy and healing. The relationship between a child and their pet is a great bond, as both accept each other for who they are. Often adults remember this relationship and bring this bond with them into adulthood. This connection may be with the same pet as in earlier times or perhaps with a similar pet later in life.

A pet can be a great teacher, as it has the ability to teach patience, responsibility, and how to accept love.

The healing relationship between a pet and an owner can be very strong and a valuable asset in difficult situations. The pet will understand if the human is under stress and needs comfort and support. These animals have the ability to pick up signs that are not necessarily verbal or even visual. It is built into their energetic systems to be aware of outside stimuli that humans are not always aware of. So when a human goes through a difficult situation, their pet can and will pick up on the situation and will sense when is the proper time to intercede to bring healing to its human partner.

Oftentimes a pet will situate itself close to the human in need and often even touching them. They may lie next to them or even on them, but usually within a short distance of the human who is under stress. A pet can also sense illness within a human's body and will respond in a similar manner when they realize the human needs their assistance, even if it's just being close to them.

When this action takes place, there is an energy that builds within the pet that will be shared with the human in hopes of releasing a chemical reaction in the human body to relieve the stress and burden the human is going through at that time. The animal will project this energy toward the human on a wavelength that may not be recognized by the pet owner at that time. However, people are able to sense when their pet is interacting with them in this manner. Perhaps during an illness or a "down day," as you say, you'll notice your pet being closer to you or even being more sedate than usual. The pet is picking up your energy, interpreting it, and sending out its healing energy in order to help you become more balanced.

Pets have a great deal of knowledge and insight into their owner's makeup. They spend vast amount of time studying and learning about their owner. This is not just to obtain food, sleep, and basic shelter, but also to learn of the nuances of their owner's energy patterns. It is one of the methods animals have that facilitate living alongside their human partner. So, they are constantly studying their environment and those who are in charge of their care.

One of the basic functions of the human-pet relationship is the acceptance of each other without judgment. The human is more apt to put restrictions on such a relationship than the pet. The pet accepts the human for who they are and does not expect certain attributes that are not relevant to the relationship. They don't care what car you drive, what you look like, or how you dress—their focus is on the interaction with them: how you treat them, how you assist with their daily living, and how you react to them when you're around. The pet can feed off this energy, recycle it, and return it to its owner with its own loving energy attached to it.

If someone has a pet, it is a good idea to seek comfort when going through the loss of a loved one as well as during illnesses or any type of sudden change in their life. The reality of the connection between the two partners is that healing can take place when that simple connection is made. Realize that the animal has this ability to bring balance and healing into your life and give them the opportunity to use their energy to help you through troubling times. It is one more avenue for you to use on your healing journey, as it can help you at a deeper level while you also share your love for your pet.

The love that is transferred between the pet and human is reinforced, which increases its strength, and should be utilized when necessary. It's a simple method of acceptance of love without judgment. There is no special practices or insights you need to be able to accept this loving energy from a pet.

We do not limit this to just a typical pet such as a dog or cat, but also any animal that has become accustomed to being with a human on a daily basis. Some lower forms of animals that may not seem to interact at will with you are still able to give off some healing energy, even though they might not be aware of such an ability. We see this with certain pets such as a goldfish, a turtle, or even a pet snake. The higher, more aware species of pets will make their energy and love more apparent because there is more interaction within the partnership. Either way, use this relationship as another tool in your quest for peace and healing.

Coping Mechanisms

Joe, there are various techniques for bringing oneself into balance that humans have access to. These techniques include the use of creativity, the ability to focus on an action that one enjoys, and participation in group activities.

All of these methods allow an individual to refocus their attention onto other stimuli. By this, we mean their focus of attention is taken away from their grief and suffering, and brought to an activity they enjoy.

These activities are healing in themselves, as they allow the body to become more balanced and relieve some of the chemical reactions the individual is experiencing at that time. In your medical terms, some will lower blood pressure as well as increase pain-relieving chemicals that are produced in the human brain.

On a psychological level, the mind is given a relief from the ongoing repetitive nature of grief. Grief has a way of becoming all-encompassing, and with these tools, that cycle can be disrupted for a significant amount of time. When an individual is involved in any of these activities, they are able to transform their physiological reaction into something that brings relief.

Many people already participate in a variety of these tools during their everyday life. These activities are natural ways of relieving stress and providing a more fulfilling outlook on life.

Many techniques can be used in this manner. One of the group activities is playing sports or even just viewing a competition. Not only is the individual refocusing their attention, but they are also sharing in the energy of many others. One does not have to be physically located close to the others to enjoy and benefit from this particular method.

Others prefer individual methods that do not involve others such as gardening, painting, and writing. All of these methods focus on the individual and involve concentration on a particular activity. While group activities involve joining energies, many individual activities can be just as powerful and healing.

A combination of these two can be utilized through the act of hobbies. They can be individual activities and can also involve a group if the individual wishes to participate. We see this with people who often enjoy working on older cars by themselves but then, at a later date, showcasing these vehicles with many other hobbyists. In this case, they are using both methods to create joy and healing in their lives. This combination method can also be used with many of the individual methods. It's up to each person to decide whether they wish to join a group after participating in the individual activity.

When these activities play out in response to relieving grief, they become more powerful, as they can create a more dynamic change in one's outlook on life. The relief, even temporary, that they bring can alter an individual's physiological makeup to the point of being able to see that there are other means and joys available to them after the loss of a loved one.

So, these types of techniques work on multiple levels, both

physiologically and on a spiritual level. By this, we mean that by indulging in these techniques, one can become more in tune with their life plan and continue on their path of learning and teaching. They are great equalizers and should be utilized throughout one's life but especially during the grieving process. They also open the connections to one's guides and loved ones who wish to send healing energy. Many times grief can hinder the connection to spirit, but by pursuing such activities, one can reinforce this connection. Spirit may give hints and inspiration where creativity is being used as it has throughout history.

One may invite a grieving person into one of these activities in order to show them that there are options to their current state of being. In doing so, you may plant a seed that an individual can learn to enjoy something for the first time that had not been expected — something they may use for the rest of their life to bring relief and joy.

So, whatever the technique you wish to pursue, it makes no difference as long as you utilize this way of healing. We hope people realize the power of healing that can be gained through simple activities that most people enjoy throughout their daily lives. So, take the time to reach out to others and ask them about the activities they enjoy, and perhaps find something you have always wanted to try but never found the time or reason.

Nature

Nature's powers have the ability to rebalance the human system. The energy that nature gives off has a healing effect on the human body—physically, emotionally, and even spiritually.

The physical Earth contributes to the species, not only for food, medicine, and shelter but also for more complex needs that many don't even realize are available. The energy that the planet gives off can be understood and accepted by an individual's own energy field. It's a partnership that is there to strengthen the mind-body connection when you have disrupted it through your actions or thoughts. It's a natural medicine cabinet that produces physical medicine and also heals the energy system.

Throughout the ages, many cultures have used nature to integrate with their systems, both community-wise and individually. They realized that the power of nature could affect the human system on many levels. That connection is still available to all today. You can utilize nature's healing powers by just thinking of it. Someone could be homebound and still have access to its powers, such as by opening a window and hearing the birds or just feeling the temperature of the air. The different smells of the seasons are strong reminders of who you are and how you are integrated into this world of balance. The power of memory can be tapped into to remind yourself of past experiences with nature, and this can switch on the healing connection even if it's impossible to go outdoors.

By being out in nature, you realize that nature is not presumptuous or fake. It's the poster for the saying "It is what it is." On a deeper level, you understand that nature is the grand caretaker of this planet. Its strength is undisputed, and there is a feeling of awe of its beauty and power. By sitting still in nature, you allow the Earth to harmonize with your being and create a true connection to your essence. This is where the healing takes place.

Nature will remind you that all your worries and drama have no place in your life. It will remind you that only today counts and that things can and do change in a minute. But it also reminds you that it is there for you to be nurtured by it and to enjoy its nonjudgmental relationship with everyone on this material planet.

Take advantage of nature. It is part of who you are, and it can fuel you with insights and balance if you take the time to utilize it properly.

Music

Throughout human history, music has been used within various cultures to instigate healing to both the mind and body. Music, which is a version of sound healing, has become more prevalent in today's societies and is an easily accessible form to utilize for healing.

The vibrational patterns that exist in various forms of music can be tuned to the human energy systems. By doing this, the connection is made on a deeper cellular level as well as reaching a level of your consciousness where it can relieve and rebalance any disturbance created by overstimulation, such from stress or emotional overload.

Many people listen to music to relax without realizing it as a natural healing method available to the human biological system. Music has the ability to put the human mind into a healthy altered state. Its vibrational patterns can awaken different parts of the body. For example, dance music can activate the motor skills, and instrumental music can create a deeper, more self-aware state.

When an individual enters an altered state in this manner, they can access parts of themselves that their consciousness may have blocked during everyday life. Daydreaming is similar in altering one's state of consciousness. And that, too, is a state where healing can occur.

Healing takes place during most forms of music, depending on the individual and the length of the exposure to it. This will determine the physiological outcome.

Some types of music are more effective at healing than others, as some can affect the human system in a negative way. By this, we mean that listening to a particular song or rhythm may cause the vibrational pattern of an individual to become agitated or angry, or even create despair. These types of effects vary wildly and can be seen in the outcome of the individual who has been exposed to them. We do not wish to judge anyone, as many of these instances have other outside interactions at play, such as environmental, interpersonal, or involving group dynamics.

So, take advantage of this method of healing to rebalance and relieve the stresses of everyday life. It's there to be utilized and should be used whenever it is needed.

Sign Stories

Music

I'd had my daughter Camilla by the time this particular instance of contact occurred. One day, I was home with Camilla, who must have been eight months old at the time. I was having a challenging day with her, and my sister began crossing my mind. I recall mentally expressing to Karla how much I wished she were still here to experience her being an aunt to my daughter and to watch them together. As tears began welling up in my eyes, I recall I had music shuffling through YouTube. Out of the blue, "I'm Yours" by Jason Mraz came on, which wasn't a song I listened to regularly, by any means. I knew this was my sister giving me a sign and letting me know that although the human side of me couldn't experience that, she was still alongside us.

In memory of Karla

Author

By mentally wishing her sister to be there to experience being an aunt, she had invited Karla to connect with her. With music playing, it was the perfect method to gain her attention. She recognized the sign immediately, so there is a high probability that other signs will be sent through songs as well.

The Blue Jay & Cardinal

This year, I began having odd encounters with animals. I've always considered myself in touch with nature, but things began occurring in ways they never had previously. I began seeing a blue jay and a cardinal show up at my house nearly daily. They would sing outside my bedroom window, take baths in the puddles, and show up at times when I was thinking about my sister, Karla, or my grandfather. One day while I was studying for finals, I saw a blue jay sit right outside the window of the room in which I was studying. Knowing these are rather solitary birds, I looked up blue jays out of curiosity as to why they were coming around. I came across a spirituality website that explained that a blue jay may represent a female energy we may have in spirit—one of resilience, independence, and uniqueness in spirit, which describes my sister to a T. I also came across a cardinal description that explained the symbolism as a male energy in spirit, one that constantly looks over us. I was taken aback, as I realized that all the signs I'd received while thinking of Karla and my grandfather were them letting me know they were right there. A couple of weeks later, the day before my daughter's second birthday, I asked my sister if she could be there with us and asked for a sign. Before I brought my daughter outside to give her a birthday present, a blue jay flew out of the attached garage. We have no birdseed or food there, so I was shocked to find it that close to the house. A few days later, a cardinal flew into my kitchen, and I had to chase it out. It kept flying from cabinet to cabinet until finally it flew out the door. A few weeks went by, and my dad was coming by to drop off my daughter's birthday gift. Once more, I asked if my sister could be present and give us a sign. While we were in the backyard enjoying my daughter spark up over her new miniature horse, I thought of my sister since horseback riding was always something she, my dad, and I did together. So much had changed since then, and I wished I could feel the three of us doing what we'd once enjoyed again. I thought of the sign I asked for and figured that my sister may have been busy in spirit or that I may have missed a sign because I was so caught up with my daughter. I'd told my dad about the encounters with birds over the last few weeks, but he seemed hesitant to believe in them. Right as I figured I would just have to trust that she had been there at some point, I looked up and there was a blue jay sitting on one of the wooden boards of the horse's stall. I pointed the bird out to my dad, and it was evident that it was bittersweet for him, too. The bird stared back at us for a few minutes before it flew away. Personally, I understood that my sister was delivering the sign I had asked for the previous day, and I thanked her and the bird for the encounter. Now, every time I see a blue jay or a cardinal oddly out of place around me, I know my people are nearby.

In memory of Karla

Author

Birds are common method of contact for spirit to let us know they're around us. Birds have been used for hundreds of years and very are easily accepted. The fact that she noticed when a blue jay or cardinal was "oddly out of place" adds to her knowing that those were true signs.

A Favorite Artist

My son gave us many signs as the days progressed. I just noted these signs without paying much attention. On the first monthly death anniversary, we had organized a devotional program of a very popular artist he listened to on his last day on this earth. I was amazed to have gotten a booking with this artist, who was booked up at least six months in advance. Over and above this, it had been raining very heavily since the week before the program, and I was worried that it would not happen as planned and that the artist would not be able to make it to the venue. The day of the program, it stopped raining in our area. Things went very smoothly, and all of us had a very spiritual experience.

In memory of my son, Smayan

Author

Here is another example of how our deceased loved ones can rearrange schedules in order to make connections that are requested. Booked times become available, cancellations pop up, and other unforeseen circumstances make previously unavailable time slots open up.

Go Team & "21"

We were at one of our favorite spots. I was thinking of my son, and I noticed a young man walk in the door. He ordered a drink, took a cozy out of his pocket, and put it on his drink. I thought it was a little odd; not many people would bring a cozy with them when they go out. It piqued my curiosity, so of course I had to ask him what the design was on his cozy. It was a Philadelphia Eagles Super Bowl Championship cozy. My son's favorite team! (We live in New England. There aren't too many Eagles fans around here.) I then introduced myself and well, of course, his name is Kevin. My son's name is Kevin. I am so thankful that my son sends me such amazing signs!

We went on an overnight stay to help relax since my son Kevin's "angelvesary" was the following day. I was thinking of him as we were checking in. We went into the room, and as I went to pick up a bottle of water, I dropped it and found a tag on the floor. It said "Forever 21" and definitely wasn't ours. Kevin passed at age twenty-one, and the date was December 21. I miss my son so very much, but these signs I receive from him are always so amazing, and he always knows when they are needed the most.

Jen, in memory of my son, Kevin

Author

In this case, it's the use of two signs that makes the connection successful. By themselves, the signs that he was using may have gotten lost, so he used the combination of his favorite team and his first name to make the connection more powerful and thus successful.

Anniversaries are always a time when we think of our loved ones in spirit, and they know this. So Kevin combined the numbers 21, his age at passing, with the date, the 21st, and then added Forever 21 to pull together a recurring number sign. He'll probably use this type of sign in the future, as it was well recognized and appreciated.

Feathers

Aymen's biggest sign for me is feathers. I find feathers everywhere. They even fall out of the sky from nowhere.

One day I was taking my (Catholic nonbeliever) Mother shopping. As we were walking into the store, she found a feather. I told her it was from Aymen. She said how could Aymen send me a feather?

When we went into the store, I texted my sister and told her Mom found a feather. My sister texted back and said, "Tell Aymen to start sending money since he sends so many feathers."

We finished shopping, and as we were walking to the car, my mother found a $5 bill! I told her what my sister had said, and she said she was going to tell Aymen to send her more money!

From nonbeliever to believer!

In memory of Aymen Soussi
By his mother, Tracy Soussi

Author
This is an example of sending a sign with the intention of opening up the idea of the possibility of our loved ones sending us signs. It was done to bring attention to the nonbeliever through something she could agree on —finding

money. It would not be unusual for someone in that position to now start receiving feathers as a sign—something she could share with her daughter and open up a more in-depth discussion of the afterlife.

The Red Light

Emma was an extremely active girl, and one of her great loves was mountain biking. That year, we decided to celebrate Christmas on Christmas Eve, which was fortuitous, as Emma became very ill on Christmas Day and had to be admitted to the ICU. One of the presents I gave her, which never made it onto her bike, was a bright brake light, as she was getting to that stage where she was beginning to ride the bike at dusk. So I gave her the present so she would have a double brake light. After she passed, I placed the brake light in the cupboard underneath the sink with a few other things for storage.

I've always had this thing about doors being shut properly because I've run into a few of them, so I know the kitchen cupboard door was definitely closed. But I was awakened by a solid red light beaming into my bedroom. That is significant because to get a solid red light on the brake light you have to go through two other programs, and it's very difficult since you have to press on it very firmly. The first program is a flashing red light, the next program is a fast blinking red light, and the next program is the solid red light. That's what woke me up. So I know now that it was definitely a sign from Emma because it's very Emma-ish and I couldn't miss it.

Karyn, in memory of Emma

Author

Emma used an object that her mother knew was connected directly to her. There was no need to use the extra energy on some random object to send the sign. Remember, our loved ones want to keep it simple, as our attention at times can be overwhelmed with things in our daily lives. So they will focus on shared memories, objects, and even sayings.

The Announcement

My son Sean, when he was on the Earth plane, worked at a local grocery store as a bagger. He'd been there through high school and then moved on to other prospects. A few years after he passed, I went into the market for the first time. I was emotional and kept talking to him in my head, saying, "Oh, there's so and so," an older manager he used to joke to me about. As I went around getting what I needed, I felt overwhelmed. As I was picking up my bag to leave the market (it is a little specialty shop, not a big grocery store), I heard over the loudspeaker, "Sean, pick up on one. Sean, you have a phone call. Pick up on one." I know that was him letting me know he was around.

In memory of my wonderful son, Sean Stigberg-Mellman

Author

The timing of a sign can mean the difference between one we recognize and one that doesn't make the connection. In this case, Sean used not only his name over the loudspeaker but also the fact that it was used in the actual store he had worked in. This is one of those "in your face" signs—loud and clear.

Final Word

I'd like to thank everyone who took the time to read this book and hopefully took something away from it that could help them heal.

We covered a lot of territory in this edition, much of it complex in nature. I noted in the beginning that I wanted to keep it as simple as possible so everyone could understand the insights that were coming through. I believe I have done that, even though many questions still remain.

As stated in the text, we don't have all the answers, and in fact we're not allowed to have all the answers while on the Earth plane. But what I wanted to do was to give you insights into the bigger picture that surrounds all of our lives.

Some of the topics can be easily understood, while others may bring up more questions than they answer. And that's okay because we're all at different levels of development. I wanted this book to be able to touch as many people as possible, regardless of where they are in their spiritual lives.

In order to do that, I have included certain topics that many other authors have shied away from. But these are the things we have questions about, the things in the back of our minds, the things that need to be asked. We might not have the full picture, but hopefully I have given you a glimpse into how our existence plays out.

Continue to study, seek out knowledge, and pass it on to others to help them understand and to help them create a more loving and insightful life.

Remember, we are *Always Connected*.

Soul Reference Guide

Soul Plans
The soul's objectives are planned out before birth with guides and groups of souls in order for certain learning experiences to take place. The soul plan will include certain achievements and opportunities that the soul will wish to accomplish while being incarnate.

Life Plan
The life plan is more of a free will decision-making objective. The soul plan cannot be overridden by the life plan. In the life plan, an individual soul may choose to make its own decisions involving how a potential learning experience will play out.

Access Points
Access points are the times/experiences when certain influences will come into one's life in order for them to grow and experience the necessary knowledge that they are seeking.

Exit Points

Exit points are created before one comes to the Earth plane. Exit points involve the ability for the soul to return to its original environment at a preselected time. These exit opportunities can be close together or spread throughout one's life cycle. If a soul has achieve the majority of the lessons it came here to experience, it may decide to return earlier than what had been planned.

Reference Quotes to Help You Heal

Bigger Picture

- *"Overall, the soul plan will include multiple opportunities for growth experiences throughout the individual's life. These opportunities may be grouped into different categories, for example, health issues, relationship issues, and situational growth experiences."*

- *"In the life plan, an individual soul may choose to use its free will to make a decision involving a potential learning experience as it sees fit. By this, we mean you alone may choose the path to take, depending on the variables that your human body is awakened to."*

- *"It is important that we start at the beginning and help you understand that the process of life is a continuation—it does not start when you're born on the Earth plane. It has begun many lengths of time before that."*

- *"So, it is not the length of time in an individual's life that determines the person's path; rather, it's the quality of life and experiences that have been planned out that must be taken into consideration."*

- *"This is the concept of free will—the ability to change one's direction while living on the Earth plane while still completing the lessons and acquiring the knowledge needed for the soul's growth and understanding of the higher concepts of love and compassion."*

- *"The age of the individual is not correlated with their ability to create experiences for growth and understanding of love and compassion."*

- *"If a soul has achieved the majority of its lessons that it came here to experience, it may decide to return earlier than had been planned."*

- *"Each soul is given several exit point opportunities to be used at the discretion of that individual soul. The decisions involve how different events will be used to decide if and when an exit point will be used."*

- *"When an individual comes to the Earth plane, they do not come as an individual alone—they come with souls whom they will integrate with to learn, experience, and grow. Some souls will come before the individual arrives, while others will arrive after the individual has already begun its life lessons."*

(Children's Insights)

- *"She said she was sorry for everything I had to go through. I knew it wasn't her fault—I knew she didn't have a choice, and I knew everything was supposed to happen the way it did."*

- *"So, I just wanted to let people know it's not difficult to leave the physical plane."*

- *"I was like, wow, this is what happens when you die. I wasn't in any pain at all. Actually, I was feeling very loved."*

- *"We knew that there was a bigger picture and that we all fit into it, but we didn't know the exact details at that moment."*

- *"We all just decided it would take place at that time and at that intersection."*

- *"So please don't blame anyone if it happens to someone you know. It might have been part of a bigger picture."*

- *"It's simply a time to look back at your life and see if you were good person. I didn't really care about my accomplishments—it was more about how I treated people. That was the main concern."*

- *"I could see that there was a reason for everything and why certain situations played out the way they did. Some things you would never guess."*

Guilt & Suicide

- *"As they continue to play out the feelings of guilt, it just reinforces the mind to continue with the same conclusion, even though it is not correct."*

- *"Once you understand the power that guilt can have over an individual, you can begin to see how taking away its power can bring relief and healing."*

- *"Some may feel that their actions or inaction caused the transition of the child, but it's not as simple as that. There are other complex mechanisms happening around transitions."*

- *"You did not have control over the child's transition."*

- *"But the pain that individuals put themselves through is not necessary."*

- *"When it is naturally time to cross over, you will meet up with your child and be able to relive the moments and experiences that you thought were lost."*

- *"Relieving suffering and helping others are extremely good ways to heal."*

(Children's Insights)

- *"I want to tell my mother that she shouldn't be totally focused on me and my crossing. I want to let her know that I am okay and that I will be fine."*

- *"A parent who passes over to see us finds out quickly that they have made a mistake."*

- *"So, the one thing I can say to parents who are thinking about crossing over to be with their children is: don't do it. It will cause more distress to you and also to others left behind. Your expectations will not be fulfilled, and you'll actually be giving up opportunities for us to share together at a later time."*

- "We will get to see each other and experience events together once again after you have passed and have fulfilled your life's obligations."

- "I'll see you when you get here after a long and interesting life. Love you, and I'll be keeping an eye on you… so behave!" (Says with a laugh)

- "We don't wish to see you judging yourself in this way."

Relationships

- "A child's passing can acutely reorient a group's dynamics. This may occur within an immediate family or among friends, colleagues, or even strangers. For all those concerned, it creates a new dynamic for growth."

- "The sibling who has lost a brother or sister or perhaps even a cousin or friend not only has to deal with the loss itself but also deal with a parent, relative, or other caretaker who's dealing with the same loss."

- "Some may come across as uncaring, but that is simply the level that they are currently at."

- "So someone who did not have children can and does get affected when one of their friends, colleagues, or loved ones loses their child. Many times people don't realize this."

- "By interacting with others who have shared this loss, you can begin to heal yourself."

- *"Oftentimes siblings may isolate themselves and begin to show signs of hiding their feelings or deepening their pain. This is something that other siblings as well as the parents should keep an eye on so it does not create more problems in the physical world."*

- *"The true meaning of life is to share the joy, happiness, and love that we all create throughout our lives."*

(Children's Insights)

- *"So, there's plenty of time for fun. I can play games with my friends, and I can watch other people perfecting their skills, like doing music, learning building skills, and studying medicine."*

- *"I just want to let you know that we are busy on this side working on things that we enjoy and that can also bring us great fun and peace as well as ways to help people on your side."*

- *"When I came to this side, I realized that my disability is something I wanted to share with others when I was alive on the Earth plane. I decided before I was born that I would take on this disability in order for others to learn how to deal with people who are not like themselves."*

- *"My life is an example of this; some situations were preplanned and, as I mentioned, my adoptive mother used her free will to take on the experience of adopting a child."*

- *"I wanted to bring this up so people understand that losing a child can be extremely devastating to nonbiological parents. Many times adults will have to hide their grief out of reasonable fear that they will be judged."*

Transitioning

Illness

- *"By this, we mean that an illness can be preplanned for certain experiences and lessons, and it can also be preplanned to be a flexible opportunity that can be utilized if needed."*

- *"Sometimes the illness can be used as an exit point after the individual has acquiring all the needed experiences they wished to accomplish in this lifetime."*

- *"An illness creates a very flexible situation that can be moved around from one age to another, from one degree to another, and from one length to another."*

Violence/Murder

- *"On a deeper level, they are already connected to their loved ones on the other side."*

- *"The main idea we wish to pass along is that the child is never alone during this transition. From the moment the decision has been made that a transfer will occur, the child is surrounded with loving support and compassion."*

- *"The child is not capable of suffering through the transition, as the process is one of compassion, love, and understanding."*

- *"A child of any age will have this information embedded in their soul so that when it is time for their crossing, they are fully aware of the procedure."*

- *"The more traumatic the passing, the more love the child will try to send back to the Earth plane. This can be done through memories, laughter, and even signs at the proper time."*

- *"The transition will be the same, as the manner in which the body has ceased to exist does not equate with a more traumatic crossing."*

- *"We have been asked if the act of murder is a preplanned event for those involved. Our answer is that no preplanning of this nature would involve an event such as murder."*

Abortion & Miscarriage

- *"The opportunity for birth may reside with the parents, but the decision about the actual birth resides with the child."*

- *"It is the soul who decides when and how it will incarnate, and it will also decide if that incarnation needs to be abruptly stopped or even terminated soon after birth."*

- *"The soul does not necessarily connect with the physical child at birth. Sometimes the connection is made during the pregnancy and at other times after the physical birth has taken place."*

- *"So, we want your readers to understand that there should be no shame or guilt with the ending of a pregnancy. There are reasons at play that neither the mother nor society realizes at that particular time."*

Addiction

- *"That may be caused by a physical ailment or a psychological situation the individual is trying to deal with. The cause of the stress can be complex or simple."*

- *"As an individual becomes more isolated in their addiction, the addiction takes on more power to control the individual on a soul level."*

- *"This search for any answers to the problems they are currently experiencing feeds the addiction cycle to the point of taking over the human experience."*

- *"We know that oftentimes people may experiment with illicit drugs or even prescription medications and cause their own transition by mistake. This act falls into the category of free will."*

- *"Many individuals have come to the Earth plane with the idea that an addiction could be a path to learning. This is true, to a certain extent, and there are many who have taken this on in their life."*

- *"So, there is a spiritual component to the activity of addictions as well as the aspect of falling into its grasp through free will."*

(Children's Insights)

- "My intention was to become stronger, but I didn't know that I needed to work on the inner me more than my physical body."

- "People don't get it when we try to hide away, but what we're trying to do is shelter ourselves from the pain we have on many different levels."

- "Some of us accidentally overdosed and were not addicted to drugs at all."

- "Education is really helpful to many, as it opens up the thoughts of other possible ways around the addiction path."

- "We realize we didn't have the tools to deal with the situations when we were living with you. We understand why we did what we did. There is no blame."

- "We help each other over here, and we help you guys a lot over there. Believe me, we have a lot of work to do, ha ha."

- "The last thing we want to see on our side is our parents suffering because of our mistakes."

- "I just hope I can help some parents understand that it's not always how things appear to be. There can be a lot more involved in passing over from an addiction."

Signs

- *"If one recognizes that a sign is possibly from a deceased loved one, it opens the lines of communication to the point where acceptance—that is, belief—can be achieved."*

- *"Everyday signs that occur to millions of people have been practiced, sharpened, and then perfected over time."*

- *"So, there are different ways of communicating from our side to yours using various methods, including animals, smells, sounds, music, and so on."*

- *"Daydreaming is a great way for us to gain access to your consciousness, too, as it's a form of meditation. Your busy mind is slowed down, and a loved one can use this time to make contact. So to all the people who say they have trouble meditating, practice daydreaming."*

- *"By sending the signs, the children make clear that their awareness of the events that are going on in their parents' lives are current, and they can be a part of those events."*

- *"Oftentimes, we doubt ourselves about whether we have actually received a sign, even though we might be open to the possibility and truly believe that we can receive a sign. Often this will reduce the quality of that sign when you accept it. The strong, loving connection is weakened by your doubt."*

- *"We are not limited as to the methods of contact, and we have vast interacting abilities within the physical plane."*

- *"So the signs will be customized for each of us, depending on our shared memories and experiences with the past loved one."*

- *"There are many reasons that we as individuals do not receive a particular sign. Some of these reasons may be due to deep grief, stress, and even because of limitations put on us for cultural and religious reasons."*

(Children's Insights)

- *"Mom understands that the feelings she gets are coming from me, but she still has doubts."*

- *"When they're feeling stressed or hateful about something, even just being stuck in traffic, it can block us from coming through."*

- *"We can hear you guys and we can feel you. Let yourselves do the same for us. It's okay to cry about us, but don't think we're not here, because we are."*

- *"And it really helps if they're having fun because the energy around them becomes finer, so it's easier for us to send a sign. When they're not having fun, their energy is denser."*

- *"I love it when I get to send a sign; it's so cool. I get to pick the time and how it's going to be done. I have so much fun deciding how I want to make my presence known."*

- *"He thinks it's okay to send signs, but he doesn't want to upset anyone he left behind."*

- *"There are lots of kids over here who, like me, love giving signs. You just have to be open to them and realize it's possible."*

- *"When she's happy, I like to be around her because I get to laugh with her. So Mom, try to be happy so I can play with you more."*

- *"I just wish she would understand that I'm right there talking to her as she's talking to herself."*

- *"Mom, I know it's hard. I can feel what you're feeling, and I need you to know that I'm fine. No really, I'm fine."*

Section VIII

Resources

Books by
Joseph M. Higgins

Hello...Anyone Home?
A Guide on How Our Deceased Loved Ones Try to Contact Us through the Use of Signs

by
Joseph M. Higgins

Channeled insight and support from the author's guides and teachers will illuminate for you the steps by which the "other side" can communicate with every individual and how you can communicate with them!

- Have you ever dreamed of departed loved ones?
- Is it possible for the dead to communicate with us?
- Have you ever experienced smells, sounds, or electrical phenomena around you after the passing of a friend, family member, or colleague?

These might be signs that they are trying to contact you to let you know that they continue to be available to you. *Hello...Anyone Home?* will teach you how to understand the process by which signs are given and received after the change known as death.

"I really like how this book will make people feel more open to talking to others about the experiences they have had, are having, or will be having."
– Now Awakened | 6 reviewers made a similar statement

"I would highly recommend this book to anyone with questions concerning a loved one who has passed on and how they may be trying to speak to you."
– Susan E. Stafford | 5 reviewers made a similar statement

"It gives you a sense of hope that our loved ones are still with us, closer than we think."
– Joan | 4 reviewers made a similar statement

Available at amazon.com and wherever books are sold.
Available on E-readers

The Everything Guide to Evidence of the Afterlife:
A scientific approach to proving the existence of life after death (Everything Series)

by
Joseph M. Higgins & Chuck Bergman

Is there life after death? Or is the end of our physical existence really the end of us? In this thought-provoking guide, you will examine scientific evidence so you can decide for yourself whether or not there is an afterlife. Medium Joseph M. Higgins and "Psychic Cop" Chuck Bergman attempt to answer questions like:

- Does consciousness survive death?
- Is communication possible between the living and the dead?
- Are mediums real—or frauds?
- What happens to us during near-death experiences?
- Where do we go when we die?
- Are heaven and hell actualities?
- What is life like after death?
- Is reincarnation real—and does everyone reincarnate?

Including an overview of various religious afterlife traditions, *The Everything Guide to Evidence of the Afterlife* introduces you to the unlimited possibilities of what we face after our release from the physical world.

Available at amazon.com and wherever books are sold.
Available on E-readers

Always Connected
For Veterans
Deceased Vets Give Guidance from the Other Side

by
Joseph M. Higgins

Real Answers to Tough Questions

- Who Are You When You Return from War?
- Why Am I Alive and Not Them?
- Will I Ever Find Peace?
- How Will God Judge Me?

Questions veterans and their families have asked since the beginning of time are answered by vets who have been there and now have passed to the other side.

With their new perspective, they reach back to help their fellow soldiers heal and gain peace with thought-provoking answers to some of the most commonly asked questions affecting veterans today.

> *I highly recommend this book, especially to those with family in the military. It addresses so many concerns that people in the military may have about the afterlife and how their actions will affect their afterlife. Very well written and easy to read.*
> – Karl Johnson

Available at amazon.com and wherever books are sold.
Available on E-readers

I Got Your Message!
Understanding Signs from Deceased Loved Ones

by
Joseph M. Higgins

The follow-up guide to *Hello... Anyone Home?* A guide on how our deceased loved ones try to contact us through the use of signs

Part of the Always Connected Series

Why millions believe in signs from beyond...and you should, too!

- What we can learn from signs
- Why people refuse to accept the signs we send them
- Why don't I get a sign?
- Can blind people get signs?
- Do children see signs more than adults?
- How believing in signs can change your life

Available at amazon.com and wherever books are sold.
Available on E-readers

Websites & Contact

Visit Joe's website for:

- Autographed books and audio ordering
- To receive discounts on future products and services
- Schedule a reading
- Always Connected jewelry
- Join the mailing list for the latest news on upcoming books, seminars, and appearances.

Joehiggins.com
Josephmhiggins.com
ACJMH.com
Alwaysconnectedcollection.com

josephmhiggins.com@gmail.com

Made in United States
North Haven, CT
16 January 2025

64535302R00163